BIKING WISCONSIN'S RAIL-TRAILS

BIKING WISCONSIN'S RAIL-TRAILS

Where to Go, What to Expect, How to Get There

by
Shawn E. Richardson

Adventure Publications, Inc.
Cambridge, MN

ADVENTURE PUBLICATIONS, INC.
P.O. Box 269
Cambridge, MN 55008
1-800-678-7006

BIKING WISCONSIN'S RAIL-TRAILS
Where to Go, What to Expect, How to Get There

First Printing 1997

ISBN # 1-885061-22-6

Text, research, cartography, & photography by Shawn E. Richardson.

Edited by Dr. Harold E. Richardson and Derek J. Anderson.

Cover and interior design by Paula Roth.

Photo credits: Shawn E. Richardson.
Front Cover:
Joyce Reoch takes a break along the Sugar River State Park Trail.
Inset: A tunnel along the Elroy-Sparta State Park Trail.
Back cover:
Top photo: A beehive barn along the Elroy-Sparta State Park Trail.
Middle photo: Madison's city skyline along the Capital City State Trail.
Bottom photo: Farms and meadows along the Ahnapee State Park Trail.

This book is for Dr. Harold Edward and Antonia Calvert Richardson, Daniel L. Hasch, Steven M. Slucher, Steve Hubner, and Joyce A. Reoch for joining me in trailblazing across Wisconsin's rail-trails.

Special thanks go to Gordon Slabaugh, Steven Stirgwolt, Carrie Davis, and Augustin Comex-Leal for test riding some of Wisconsin's rail-trails.

Special thanks also go to the Rails-to-Trails Conservancy, the Wisconsin Department of Natural Resources, and all the recreationalists who will use these trails.

Contents

Introduction

I researched and created Biking Wisconsin's Rail-Trails as a guide to Wisconsin's major off-road multipurpose trails and rail-trails. It provides tourists, weekend travelers, outdoor lovers, and recreationalists with a set of uniform, detailed maps, which allow them to easily find each trail. The maps and text also help drivers find parking and alternate locations for dropping off or picking up trail users. Maps of trails with permanent mile markers help users calculate the distance of their outdoor excursions.

Most of the trails described herein have a smooth surface, allowing users to bicycle, mountain bike, walk, hike, or travel by wheelchair. Many are open to cross-country skiers and snowmobilers during the winter months, and some even allow for ATV use and horseback riding. Best of all, Wisconsin prohibits motorized vehicles from using most of the trails at any time, providing safe recreational use throughout the year. Be sure to check each individual trail to make sure it allows for your intended use.

While the book does not include maps for many of the shorter or limited-use trails, a description of each trail can be found under "Wisconsin's Unimproved Surfaced Rail-Trails" on page 117. Addresses are provided so readers can obtain more information concerning these trails.

The maps and information in Biking Wisconsin's Rail-Trails are current as of 1997. Future editions will include trails currently under development, a list of which appears under "Wisconsin's Potential Rail-Trails" on page 121. If you find that any of the maps need corrections, or if you have discovered trails not listed, write to me at: Shawn E. Richardson, Biking USA's Rail-Trails, PO Box 284, Hilliard, OH 43026-0284. I hope this book makes trailblazing across the Badger State more convenient and enjoyable for you, and whenever you use these trails, always keep in mind the safety tips listed in the back of this book. Happy Trails!

–Shawn E. Richardson, 1997

The Rails-to-Trails Conservancy

Founded in 1985 with the mission of enhancing America's communities and countrysides, the Rails-to-Trails Conservancy is a national, nonprofit organization dedicated to converting abandoned rail corridors into a nationwide network of multipurpose trails. By linking parks, schools, neighborhoods, communities, towns, cities, states, and national parks, this system will connect important landmarks and create both a haven for wildlife and a safe place for able and handicapped adults and children to bicycle, walk, in-line skate, and travel by wheelchair. Rail-Trails help to meet the demand for local recreational opportunities, and connect with long-distance trails to make it possible to ride continuously across a state (and eventually even from coast to coast!) without ever encountering a motorized vehicle.

This vision of the Rails-to-Trails Conservancy is quickly becoming a reality. Over 800 trails totaling more than 8,000 miles have already been successfully converted into multipurpose trails in the United States, and another 1,000 rail-trails are in the works.

Since the opening of the 32-mile Elroy-Sparta State Park trail (Wisconsin's first rail-trail) in 1967, Wisconsin's rail-trail network has grown to include about 60 trails, and over 1100 miles. The trail network continues to grow, and Wisconsin is connecting their trails to all four of its neighboring states. Even as you read this, grassroot efforts are taking place throughout Wisconsin to convert even more miles of abandoned railroads into scenic greenways.

Your membership, support, and enthusiasm will help the Rails-to-Trails Conservancy, as well as the state of Wisconsin, continue to make their vision a reality. See page 141 for information on joining the Rails-to-Trails Conservancy.

Wisconsin Department of Natural Resources and Trail Fees

The Wisconsin Department of Natural Resources invests a large amount of money in acquiring rail corridors and transforming them into smooth surfaced bicycle trails. (It takes about as much effort to remove the rails and ties as it did to build the railroads over a century ago!) After the rails and ties are removed, bridges are planked, guard rails are erected, crushed limestone is laid and graded, and safety directional signs and mile markers are installed. There are also ongoing costs, such as maintaining the trail surfaces, bridges, and signs, not to mention the picking up of litter and debris.

To recover part of these costs, bicyclists, horseback riders, and cross country skiers age 18 and older must pay a daily, or an annual, trail admission fee. Call or write to the address or phone number below for current trail fees. An annual admission fee can be used on any of the Wisconsin State Park Trails during the year.

For more information on Wisconsin's State Parks, Forests, and Trails, or to request campground reservation forms, call or write the Wisconsin Department of Natural Resources, P.O. Box 7921, Madison, WI 53707. Or call at 608-266-2621; 608-267-6897 TDD.

You may buy admission cards by mail or in person from the Wisconsin Department of Natural Resources, State Park trail headquarters, or trail rangers along the trails.

The trails are open from 6 a.m. to 11 p.m. daily. Pets are allowed, but they must be on a leash no longer than eight feet.

State Park Trails	Length in Miles	State Trail Fee
Ahnapee	29.0	
Bearskin	18.5	X
Chippewa River	23.5	X
Elroy-Sparta	32.0	X
400	22.0	X
Gandy Dancer	48.0	X
Glacial Drumlin (East)	28.0	X
Glacial Drumlin (West)	21.0	X
Great River	24.0	X
Hillsboro	4.3	
La Crosse River	21.5	X
Military Ridge	38.0	X
Mountain Bay	83.4	X
Pecatonica	10.5	
Red Cedar	14.5	X
Sugar River	23.0	X
Wild Goose	34.0	
Wiouwash (North)	21.0	
Wiouwash (South)	20.0	

Trail Descriptions

ASPHALT OR CONCRETE – suitable for biking, mountain bicycling, hiking, in-line skating, and wheelchairs.

COARSE ASPHALT – suitable for bicycling, mountain bicycling, hiking, and wheelchairs.

SMOOTH CRUSHED GRAVEL – suitable for bicycling, mountain bicycling, hiking, and wheelchairs. During thawing and extremely wet weather, bicycles, mountain bicycles, and wheelchairs should avoid using this trail surface because the soft surface can rut easily.

COURSE CRUSHED GRAVEL – suitable for mountain bicycling and hiking.

GRASS OR DIRT – suitable for mountain biking and hiking.

ORIGINAL BALLAST – difficult for most trail users due to the size of larger rocks.

NOTE: Trail users should check conditions for each trail by contacting the trail managers listed in this book.

Legend

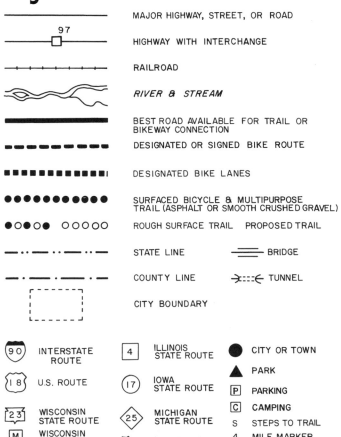

———————— MAJOR HIGHWAY, STREET, OR ROAD

—————97—————□————— HIGHWAY WITH INTERCHANGE

—+—+—+—+—+— RAILROAD

RIVER & STREAM

BEST ROAD AVAILABLE FOR TRAIL OR BIKEWAY CONNECTION

DESIGNATED OR SIGNED BIKE ROUTE

DESIGNATED BIKE LANES

SURFACED BICYCLE & MULTIPURPOSE TRAIL (ASPHALT OR SMOOTH CRUSHED GRAVEL)

ROUGH SURFACE TRAIL   PROPOSED TRAIL

STATE LINE   BRIDGE

COUNTY LINE   TUNNEL

CITY BOUNDARY

(90) INTERSTATE ROUTE	[4] ILLINOIS STATE ROUTE	● CITY OR TOWN
(18) U.S. ROUTE	(17) IOWA STATE ROUTE	▲ PARK
[23] WISCONSIN STATE ROUTE	⟨25⟩ MICHIGAN STATE ROUTE	[P] PARKING
[M] WISCONSIN COUNTY ROUTE	[60] MINNESOTA STATE ROUTE	[C] CAMPING
(I) BICYCLE ROUTE LETTER/NUMBER		S STEPS TO TRAIL
		4● MILE MARKER
		■ LANDMARK

TRAIL USE SYMBOLS:

Black symbols = trail use allowed   Gray symbols = trail use not allowed

🅂	State Trail Fee	$	Trail Fee
🚲	Bicycling	🚵	Mountain Biking
🚶	Hiking	🛼	In-line Skating
🐴	Bridal Path	🎿	Cross-county Skiing
🛷	Snowmobiling	🏍	All Terrain Vehicles
♿	Handicap Accessible		

State Map Showing Wisconsin's Trails

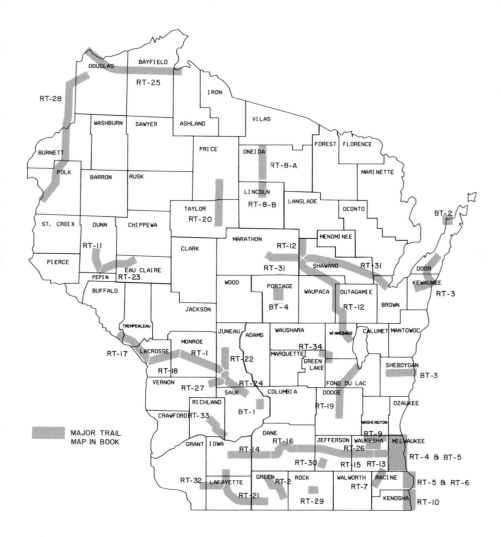

LEGEND

RT: Major rail-trail
(greater than 1 mile and/or smooth Surface trail following a former railroad)

BT: Bike trail
(smooth trail that does not follow a former railroad)

Wisconsin's Trails

Trail Name	Vicinity	Map Code	Page #
Ahnapee State Park Trail	Sturgeon Bay	RT-3	8
Aaron (Henry Aaron) State Park Trail	Milwaukee	BT-5	10
Baraboo-Devils Lake State Park Trail	Baraboo	BT-1	106
Bearskin State Park Trail	Minocqua	RT-8	22
Bugline Recreation Trail	Menomonee Falls	RT-9	26
Capital City State Trail	Madison	RT-16	48
Cheese Country Recreation Trail	Monroe/ Mineral Point	RT-21	64
Chippewa River State Park Trail	Eau Claire	RT-23	70
Elroy-Sparta State Park Trail	Elroy/Sparta	RT-1	2
400 State Park Trail	Elroy/Reedsburg	RT-24/27	72
Gandy Dancer State Park Trail	Superior/St. Croix Falls	RT-28	82
Glacial Drumlin State Park Trail	Madison/Waukesha	RT-15	44
Glacial River Trail	Fort Atkinson	RT-30	90
Great River State Park Trail	La Crosse	RT-17	52
Green Circle Trail	Stevens Point	BT-4	114
Hiawatha State Park Trail	Tomahawk	RT-8	24
Hillsboro State Park Trail	Hillsboro	RT-27/24	72
Kenosha County Bicycle Trail	Kenosha	RT-10	28
La Crosse River State Park Trail	La Crosse/Sparta	RT-18	54
Lake Country Recreation Trail	Waukesha	RT-26	80
Military Ridge State Park Trail	Madison/Dodgeville	RT-14	40
Mountain Bay State Park Trail	Green Bay/Wausau	RT-31	92
New Berlin Recreation Trail	Waukesha	RT-13	38
Oak Leaf Trail	Milwaukee	RT-4	10
Old Plank Road Trail	Sheboygan	BT-3	110
Omaha Trail	Elroy	RT-22	68

WISCONSIN'S MAJOR RAIL-TRAILS

ELROY-SPARTA STATE PARK TRAIL
VICINITY: *Elroy-Sparta*
TRAIL LENGTH: *32.0 miles*
SURFACE: *smooth crushed gravel*
TRAIL USE:

Converted from an abandoned railroad in 1967, the Elroy-Sparta State Park Trail holds the distinction of being Wisconsin's first bicycle trail. This scenic trail is 32 miles in length, and goes through the unglaciated hills and valleys of southwestern Wisconsin. Small farm and Amish farm communities can be found in Elroy, Kendall, Wilton, Norwalk, and Sparta. The Elroy-Sparta State Park Trail was originally a part of the 300-mile Wisconsin Bikeway, which was created back in 1966, and followed the quiet backroads from La Crosse to Kenosha and Racine. Today, a network of scenic rail-trails have replaced the Wisconsin Bikeway.

The Trail is known for its trestles and tunnels. The longest of the three tunnels is three-quarters of a mile long, and can be found between mile markers 7/25 & 9/23. The tunnels are very cool and dark, so you may want to bring a jacket and flashlight along. It is also suggested that you walk your bicycle through the tunnels. The tunnels are closed from mid-November until April, and snowmobilers must follow the detour signs around them.

The Elroy Sparta State Park Trail connects to three other trails. In Sparta, you can continue west along the La Crosse River State Park Trail. In Elroy, you can continue southeast along the 400 State Park Trail. You can also go north from Elroy along the Omaha Trail, although this is a county trail which requires a separate trail fee.

The trail headquarters is located inside the restored Kendall Depot. A shuttle service is available in Kendall for cyclists who want to ride only one way. All the towns along the trail have parking and restaurants.

PARKING:
Parking can be found along the trail in the towns of Elroy, Kendall, Wilton, Norwalk, and Sparta.

FOR MORE INFORMATION:
Wildcat Work Unit
P.O. Box 99, Ontario, WI 54651-0099
608-337-4775

Dr. Harold E. Richardson biking Wisconsin's oldest rail-trail.

Tunnel 3 (¾ of a mile long) near mile-marker 7/25.

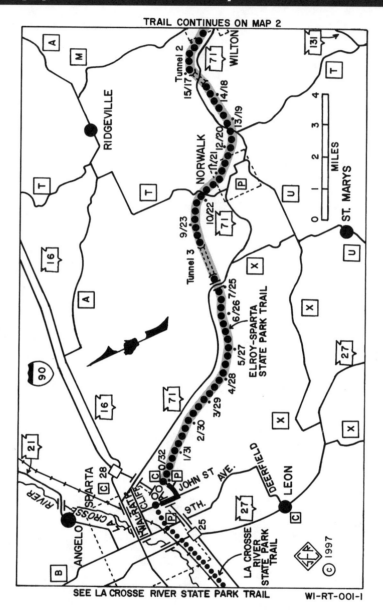

TRAIL CONTINUES ON MAP 2

SEE LA CROSSE RIVER STATE PARK TRAIL

WI-RT-OOI-I

ELROY-SPARTA STATE PARK TRAIL (MAP 1)
MONROE & JUNEAU COUNTIES
32.0 MILES
SURFACE: SMOOTH CRUSHED GRAVEL

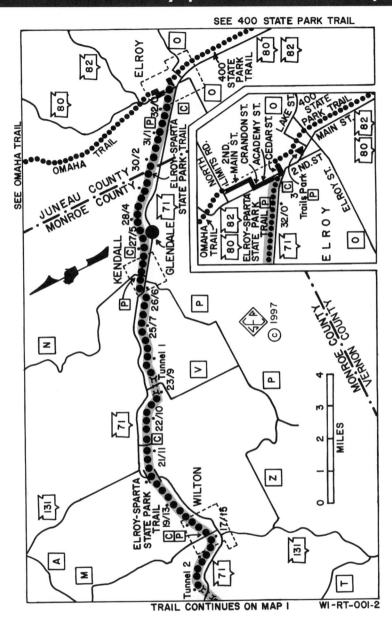

SEE 400 STATE PARK TRAIL

TRAIL CONTINUES ON MAP I   WI-RT-OOI-2

ELROY-SPARTA STATE PARK
TRAIL (MAP 2)

SUGAR RIVER STATE PARK TRAIL
VICINITY: *Broadhead/New Glarus*
TRAIL LENGTH: *23.0 miles*
SURFACE: *smooth crushed gravel*
TRAIL USE: 💲 📵 🚲 🐕 🏃 ⛺ 🐎 🏊 🏍 ♿

The Sugar River State Park Trail opened in 1972, making it Wisconsin's second oldest rail-trail. It runs 23 miles between Brodhead and New Glarus through Green County. Like the Elroy-Sparta State Park Trail, the Sugar River State Park Trail was also a part of the former 300-mile Wisconsin Bikeway.

The scenery consists of gently rolling hills, and farmland along the Sugar River Valley. The Sugar River received its name from an incident in which some pioneers accidentally lost a boat full of sugar to the river, making the water very sweet.

The main highlight along this trail is New Glarus, a town settled by Swiss immigrants. The architecture along the main streets makes you feel as if you had suddenly been transported into Switzerland.

The former Milwaukee Road depot in New Glarus serves as the Sugar River State Park Trail Headquarters. A shuttle service is also available for cyclists who wish to ride the trail one way. Another bicycle path can be taken just south of New Glarus to visit the New Glarus Woods State Park.

PARKING:
Parking can be found in the towns of New Glarus, Monticello, Albany, and Brodhead.

Former railroad headquarters in New Glarus.

FOR MORE INFORMATION:
Sugar River State Park Trail
P.O. Box 781, New Glarus, WI 53574-0781
608-527-2334

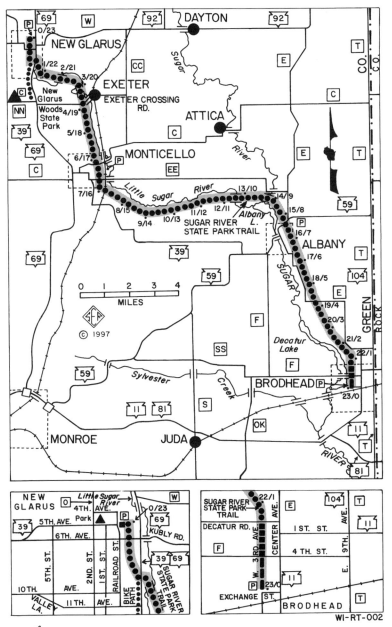

SUGAR RIVER STATE PARK TRAIL
GREEN COUNTY
23.0 MILES
SURFACE: SMOOTH CRUSHED GRAVEL

AHNAPEE STATE PARK TRAIL
VICINITY: *Sturgeon Bay*
TRAIL LENGTH: *29.0 miles*
SURFACE: *smooth crushed gravel*
TRAIL USE:

The Ahnapee State Park Trail gets its name from the Ahnapee River, which the trail parallels through Southern Door and Kewaunee Counties. In 1973, this trail became the third of Wisconsin's railroads to be converted into a bicycle trail. The trail starts in Casco and ends in Sturgeon Bay, passing through the towns of Algoma, Forestville, and Maplewood along the way.

During the 1980s and the early 1990s the maintenance of this trail suffered, due to a lack of funding. It was not until 1994 that the Wisconsin Department of Natural Resources signed an agreement that allowed Door and Kewaunee Counties to take over the maintenance of the trail.

Attractions along the trail include a wildlife area, several wetlands, the Ahnapee River Crossing, a county park near Forestville, and several views of scenic farmland. Future plans for the Ahnapee State Park Trail include extending the trail in both directions to Sturgeon Bay and Green Bay.

PARKING:
Parking can be found at both ends of the trail, and in the town of Forestville.

Farms and meadows along Ahnapee State Park Trail.

FOR MORE INFORMATION:

DOOR COUNTY SECTION:
County of Door Airport & Parks
Dept., 3418 Park Dr.
Sturgeon Bay, WI 54235
414-743-3636

KEWAUNEE COUNTY SECTION:
Algoma Area Chamber of Commerce
1226 Lake St., Algoma, WI 54201
414-487-2041

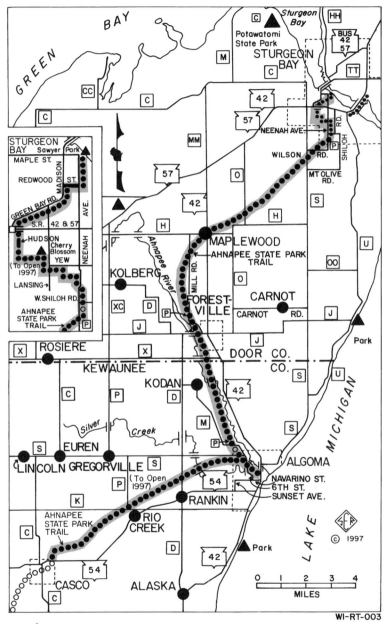

WI-RT-003

AHNAPEE STATE PARK TRAIL
KEWAUNEE & DOOR COUNTIES
29.0 MILES
SURFACE: SMOOTH CRUSHED GRAVEL

9

OAK LEAF TRAIL
VICINITY: *Milwaukee*
TRAIL LENGTH: *96.4 miles*
SURFACE: *asphalt & streets*

TRAIL USE:

AARON STATE PARK TRAIL
VICINITY: *Milwaukee*
TRAIL LENGTH: *3.5 miles*
SURFACE: *asphalt*

TRAIL USE:

The Oak Leaf Trail is a 96.4-mile loop that follows the Green Belt Park System through the four corners of Milwaukee and Milwaukee County. This lengthy bike route consists of paved trails, park roads, and streets. The scenery varies from the lakefront city skyline to the quiet parklands on the edge of Milwaukee.

The history of this trail goes back to 1939, when Harold "Zip" Morgan, a member of the League of American Wheelmen, Vice President and founder of Wisconsin Council of American Youth Hostels, working with the Optimist Club and the Milwaukee County Park Commission, created a 64-mile bike route. This route incorporated different parkways, streets, and green strips of land around the edge of Milwaukee. "Zip" would run two-day bicycle tours on this route, which included overnight stays at the former Wauwatosa Youth Hostel.

In October of 1968 the first massive one day tour was formed, which gave the event, and eventually the trail, the name "Milwaukee 64." About the same time, the first asphalt sections of the bicycle path were constructed, near downtown Milwaukee along the lake front.

In 1975, a four-mile stretch of abandoned railroad was converted into a bike path between downtown Milwaukee and Estabrook Park. In 1976, to celebrate the United States' 200th birthday, the "Milwaukee County Parks '64' Bike Tour Route" became the "Milwaukee County '76' Bike Tour Route." Seventy-six miles was such a long loop that an 11-mile East-West Connector was added to the trail. Several other spurs and loops were added to the route during the late 1970s and 1980s, making the total length of the route 96 miles.

In 1996, the "Milwaukee County Parks '76' Bike Tour Route" name was changed to its current name, the "Oak Leaf Trail." Currently, the Oak Leaf Trail is 35% off-road bike paths, 34% park roads, and 31% city streets. New bike paths and rail-trails for the Oak Leaf Trail are in the planning stages.

If your time is short and you want a scenic tour, you can enjoy a beautiful 10-mile stretch of trail along the bluffs of Lake Michigan between South Milwaukee and Milwaukee (Map 1). This separate bike path winds through Grant Park,

Oak Leaf Trail along Lake Michigan.

Children enjoy the Oak Leaf Trail through the Northwestern area of Milwaukee.

Warnimont Park, Sheridan Park, Bay View Park, and South Shore Park, with an occasional distant glimpse of the Milwaukee city skyline.

If you are in more of a "city mood," a network of bicycle trails exists, offering constant views of both Lake Michigan and the Milwaukee city skyline (Map 2). This trail offers plenty of museums, historical sites, cultural activities, summer festivals, building architecture, and scenic lakeside parks. If you travel the entire "lake loop," and are willing to climb a big hill, you'll go through a neighborhood of grand beautiful mansions along Terrace Avenue and Wahl Drive. If you're in the mood to ride faster, cross over to the west side of Lincoln Memorial Drive, near Veterans Park or O'Donnell Park, and enjoy a very smooth four mile rail-trail from downtown Milwaukee to the city of Shorewood and Estabrook Park.

If you're interested in a quick tour of Northwest Milwaukee (Map 3), there is a seven-mile stretch of bike path from the Bretzka Park Golf Course, along Bradley Road, down to Wauwatosa, where the Menomonee River Parkway starts/ends. If this ride isn't enough, follow the Menomonee River Parkway another 4.5 miles into the center of Wauwatosa, where there is a variety of shops and restaurants.

If you're interested in a quick tour of Southwest Milwaukee (Map 4), there is an enjoyable nine-mile stretch of park roads and bike paths. Starting in Greenfield Park, on Lincoln Avenue in West Allis, you can either bicycle the six-mile New Berlin Recreation Trail in Waukesha County, which intersects with the Oak Leaf Trail, or follow the Oak Leaf Trail. To follow the Oak Leaf Trail south, follow the Park road from Greenfield Park in a southerly direction to the Root River Parkway. Follow the Root River Parkway south from Lincoln Avenue to where the bike path picks up. Next, follow the bike path until the Root River Parkway picks up again, near Interstate-43. Follow the Root River Parkway past 92nd Street and Forest Home Road. A three-mile loop can be taken to explore Whitnall Park from Root River Parkway. The scenic Root River Parkway ends at Loomis Road.

Future plans for the Oak Leaf Trail include creating a network of off-road bike paths, linking the Oak Leaf Trail Network to the Racine County Bicycle Trails, the Bugline Recreation Trail in Waukesha County, and to eventually have the entire Oak Leaf Trail Network become part of the planned Green Bay to Chicago Cross State Trail.

PARKING:
Parking is available in most of the parks along the Oak Leaf Trail.

FOR MORE INFORMATION:

OAK LEAF TRAIL	AARON (HENRY AARON) STATE PARK TRAIL
Milwaukee County Parks	Wisconsin DNR, 2300 N.
9480 Watertown Plank Road	Dr. Martin Luther King Jr. Dr., Box 12436
Wauwatosa, WI 53226	Milwaukee, WI 53212-0436
414-257-6100	414-263-8711

Joyce A. Reoch relaxes along the Oak Leaf Trail in front of the Milwaukee City skyline.

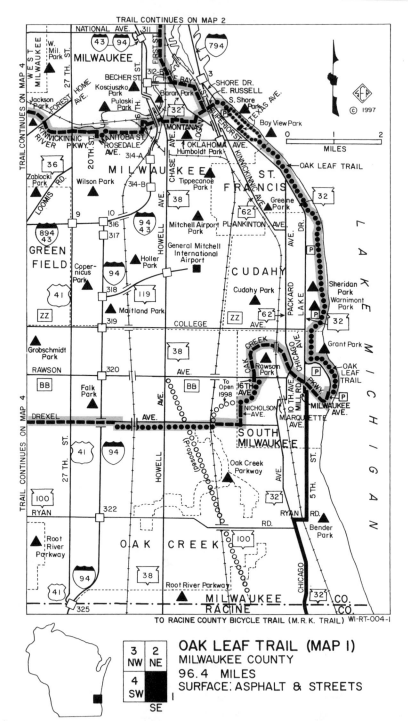

OAK LEAF TRAIL (MAP 1)
MILWAUKEE COUNTY
96.4 MILES
SURFACE: ASPHALT & STREETS

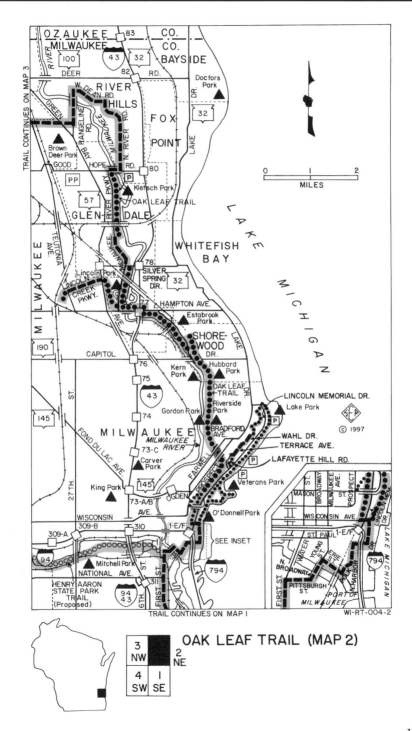

OAK LEAF TRAIL (MAP 2)

3 NW	2 NE
4 SW	1 SE

15

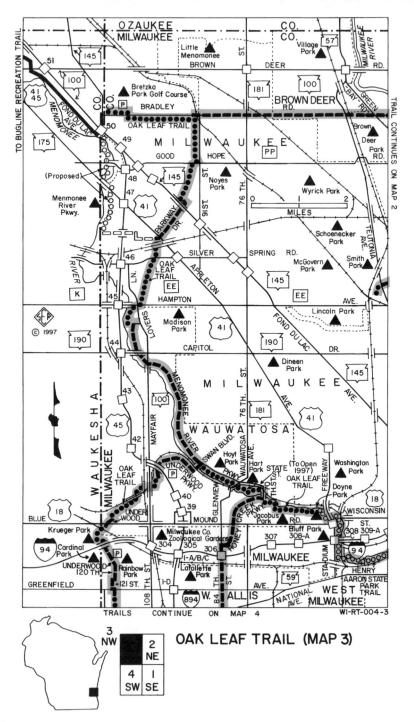

OAK LEAF TRAIL (MAP 3)

16

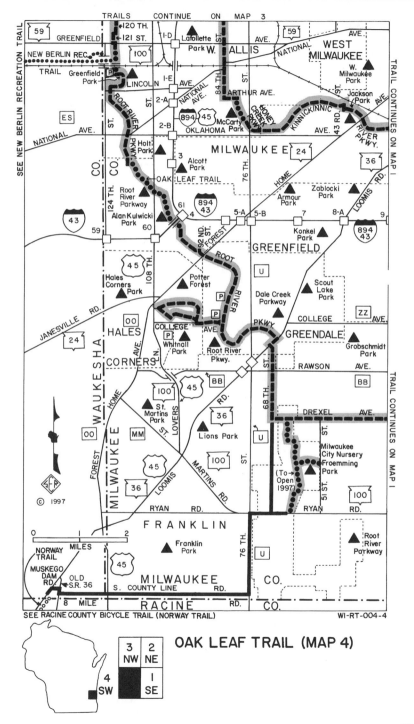

OAK LEAF TRAIL (MAP 4)

3 NW	2 NE
4 SW	1 SE

RACINE COUNTY BICYCLE TRAILS
VICINITY: *Racine*
TRAIL LENGTH: *Total of 12.0 miles*
NORTH SHORE TRAIL: *3.0 miles*
M.R.K. TRAIL: *5.0 miles*
RACINE-STURTEVANT TRAIL: *4.0 miles*
SURFACE: *smooth crushed gravel*
TRAIL USE: 🚲 🚲 🚶 🐕 ⛷ 🦽

In 1970, a 100-mile bicycle route was established through Racine County. The route followed a variety of back roads, and was a part of the former 300-mile Wisconsin Bikeway, created back in 1966. In the late 1970s, portions of the 100-mile bicycle route were put along the abandoned railroads of the Racine Area.

The three-mile Racine County Bicycle Trail (North Shore Trail) goes south of Racine into Kenosha County. Known as the Kenosha County Bicycle Trail, the 16-mile trail continues south to the state of Illinois. Cliffside Park, overlooking Lake Michigan, is a scenic attraction north of Racine, along the five-mile Racine County Bicycle Trail (M.R.K. Trail).

The Racine County Bicycle Trail (Racine-Sturtevant Trail) goes from the Racine County Bicycle Trail (North Shore Trail) in Southern Racine to Pritchard Park and Sturtevant (slated to open in 1997).

Future plans for the Racine County Bicycle Trails include linking them together through the City of Racine and connecting the Trail Network north to the Oak Leaf Trail Network in Milwaukee. The Racine County Bicycle Trail Network may also become part of the planned Green Bay to Chicago Cross State Route. A bicycle map of Racine County, showing the 100-mile bike route, may be ordered from the address below.

PARKING:
Parking is available in most parks near and along the trails.

FOR MORE INFORMATION:
Racine County Public Works Department
14200 Washington Ave.
Sturtevant, WI 53177-1253
414-886-8440

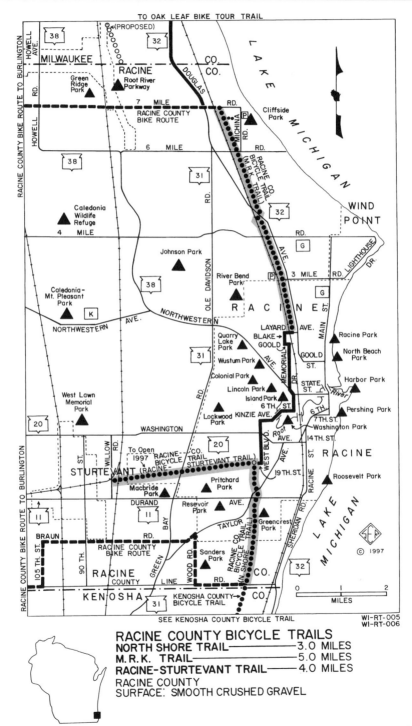

RACINE COUNTY BICYCLE TRAILS
NORTH SHORE TRAIL————————3.0 MILES
M.R.K. TRAIL————————————5.0 MILES
RACINE-STURTEVANT TRAIL——4.0 MILES
RACINE COUNTY
SURFACE: SMOOTH CRUSHED GRAVEL

19

RACINE COUNTY BICYCLE TRAILS

VICINITY: *Burlington/Waterford*
TRAIL LENGTH: *total of 10.2 miles*
Burlington Trail: 4.0 miles
Norway Trail: 1.2 miles
Waterford-Wind Lake Trail: 5.0 miles
SURFACE: *smooth crushed gravel*
TRAIL USE: 🚫 💲 🅷 🚲 🚴 🚶 🏃 🐎 🎿 🏊 🏍 ♿

In 1970, a 100-mile bicycle route was established through Racine County. It followed various back roads, and was part of the former 300-mile Wisconsin Bikeway. In the late 1970s, portions of the 100-mile bicycle route were put along abandoned railroads in the Burlington/Waterford Area.

The four-mile Racine County Bicycle Trail (Burlington Trail) starts in Riverside Park and goes north paralleling State Route-36. The trail dead ends at Fox River, and you must turn around and go back to Browns Lake Drive. Back roads may be followed north from this point to Waterford. To travel the five-mile Racine County Bicycle Trail (Waterford-Wind Lake Trail) from here, this trail goes north and also parallels State Route-36. Towards the north end of this trail, you may want to visit Meyer Park. From the north end of this trail, follow the bike route signs north along Loomis Road until you cross over State Route-36. From this intersection, the 1.2-mile Racine County Bicycle Trail (Norway Trail) goes north, following State Route-36 to the Waukesha-Racine County Line, (slated to open in 1998). From this point, it is best to turn around and go back, to avoid riding on State Route-36.

Future plans for the Racine County Bicycle Trails include connecting these three trail segments together. The trail may one day continue on into Waukesha County and connect to their trail network. A bicycle map of Racine County, showing the 100-mile bike route, may be ordered from the address shown below.

PARKING:
Parking is available in Riverside Park in Burlington and in Meyer Park, along Loomis Road, near Wind Lake.

FOR MORE INFORMATION:
Racine County Public Works Department
14200 Washington Ave.
Sturtevant, WI 53177-1253
414-886-8440

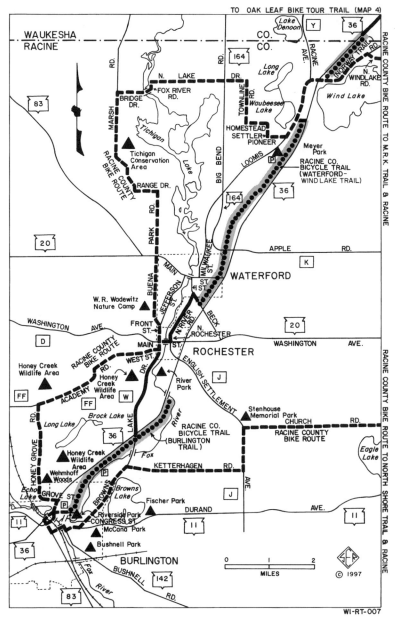

TO OAK LEAF BIKE TOUR TRAIL (MAP 4)

WAUKESHA
RACINE

WAUKESHA
RACINE

CO.
CO.

Lake
Denoon

Y

36

RACINE COUNTY BIKE ROUTE TO M.R.K. TRAIL & RACINE

164

Long
Lake

RACINE
AVE.

NORWAY TRAIL

WINDLAKE
RD.

N.

Wind Lake

N. LAKE DR.

FOX RIVER
RD.

BRIDGE
DR.

MARSH
RD.

83

TOWNLINE RD.

Waubeesee
Lake

Tichigan

HOMESTEAD
SETTLER
PIONEER

Meyer
Park

Tichigan
Conservation
Area

RACINE COUNTY
BIKE ROUTE

Lake

BIG BEND

LOOMIS

P

RACINE CO.
BICYCLE TRAIL
(WATERFORD-
WIND LAKE TRAIL)

RANGE DR.

PARK RD.

164

36

20

MILWAUKEE ST.

APPLE

RD.

K

MAIN

BUENA

JEFFERSON ST.

ST.
ST.

WATERFORD

W. R. Wadewitz
Nature Camp

N. RIVER RD.

BECK

WASHINGTON AVE.

FRONT
ST.

N.
ROCHESTER

20

D

RACINE COUNTY
BIKE ROUTE

MAIN ST.

WASHINGTON AVE.

Honey Creek
Wildlife Area

RD.

WEST ST.

ROCHESTER

LAKE DR.

ENGLISH SETTLEMENT

River
Park

J

FF

Honey
Creek
Wildlife
Area

ACADEMY

FF

W

Stenhouse
Memorial Park

CHURCH

RD.

Brock Lake

River

RACINE CO.
BICYCLE TRAIL
(BURLINGTON
TRAIL)

RACINE COUNTY
BIKE ROUTE

Long Lake

36

Fox

Eagle
Lake

Honey Creek
Wildlife
Area

HONEY GROVE RD.

Wehmhoff
Woods

P

KETTERHAGEN

RD.

Echo
Lake

GROVE ST.

P

BROWNS

Browns
Lake

Fischer Park

J

AVE.

11

Riverside Park
CONGRESS ST.

DURAND

AVE.

11

11

McCana Park

11

36

Bushnell Park

0   1   2
MILES

© 1997

BURLINGTON

BUSHNELL

142

Fox River

83

RD.

RACINE COUNTY BIKE ROUTE TO NORTH SHORE TRAIL & RACINE

WI-RT-007

RACINE COUNTY BICYCLE TRAILS
BURLINGTON TRAIL——————————4.0 MILES
WATERFORD-WINDLAKE TRAIL—5.0 MILES
NORWAY TRAIL——————————1.2 MILES
RACINE COUNTY
SURFACE: SMOOTH CRUSHED GRAVEL

21

BEARSKIN STATE PARK TRAIL
VICINITY: Minocqua
TRAIL LENGTH: 18.5 miles
SURFACE: smooth crushed gravel
TRAIL USE:

The Wisconsin Department of Natural Resources opened the Bearskin State Park Trail to the public in 1977. The Trail is named after Bearskin Creek, a tributary of the Tomahawk River. This 18.5-mile trail follows US Route-51 through the north woods of Northern Wisconsin.

Plenty of tall pine trees enhance the ride's scenic flavor. At times this dry trail seems only inches above the colorful wetlands it traverses. About three miles north of Goodnow, a "surprise hill" has been thrown into the trail; be very cautious near mile marker 7/11! There are plenty of private campgrounds and resorts located near the trail. While you will see plenty of wildlife along the Bearskin State Park Trail, you will probably not see any bears.

PARKING:
Parking can be found on the South end of the trail along County Route K, Blue Lake Road north of Hazelhurst, and on the North end of the trail in Minocqua.

The 746 Harshaw Trestle is near mile marker 2/16.

FOR MORE INFORMATION:
Bearskin State Park Trail
4125 Highway M
Boulder Junction, WI 54512
715-385-2727

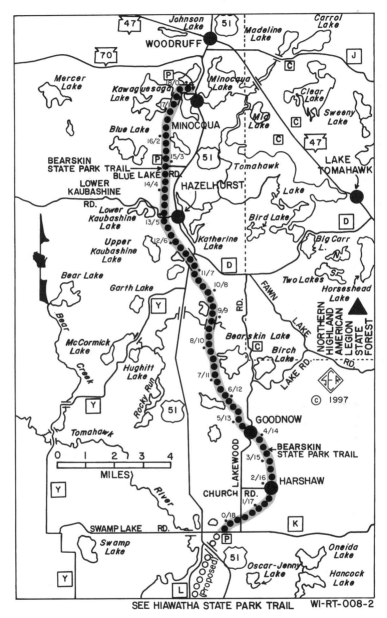

SEE HIAWATHA STATE PARK TRAIL   WI-RT-008-2

BEARSKIN STATE PARK TRAIL
ONEIDA COUNTY
18.4 MILES
SURFACE: SMOOTH CRUSHED GRAVEL

23

HIAWATHA STATE PARK TRAIL
VICINITY: *Tomahawk*
TRAIL LENGTH: *6.6 Miles*
SURFACE: *smooth crushed gravel*
TRAIL USE: 🟨 🟨 🚲 🚵 🚶 🏕️ 🐕 ⛷️ ➡️ 🏍️ ♿

In 1990, the Hiawatha State Park Trail opened. It was built by Lincoln County, who still manages the trail. The Hiawatha State Park Trail follows the same former railroad bed that the Bearskin State Park Trail follows. The south end of the 6.6-mile trail is near Sara Park on Somo Avenue, in Tomahawk. From Tomahawk, it crosses a scenic low trestle over the Wisconsin River to the north. The trail goes through Heafford Junction, and ends north of Headford Junction, on the Oneida-Lincoln County Line near Lake Nokomis.

The "Hiawatha" gets its name from a passenger train which used to bring travelers to the north woods during the 1940s and 1950s. The tall pine trees along this trail make this trail very scenic, and give the trail user the feeling of being close to nature.

Future plans for both the Hiawatha and Bearskin State Park Trails include connecting the two trails together by completing the last six-mile gap of the abandoned railroad, making one continuous 30-mile trail.

PARKING:
Parking is available in Tomahawk, near Somo Avenue in Sara Park.

Hiawatha State Park Trail crosses the Wisconsin River.

FOR MORE INFORMATION:
Hiawatha State Park Trail
Lincoln County Forestry Land & Parks, Courthouse Building
Merrel, WI 54452
715-536-0327

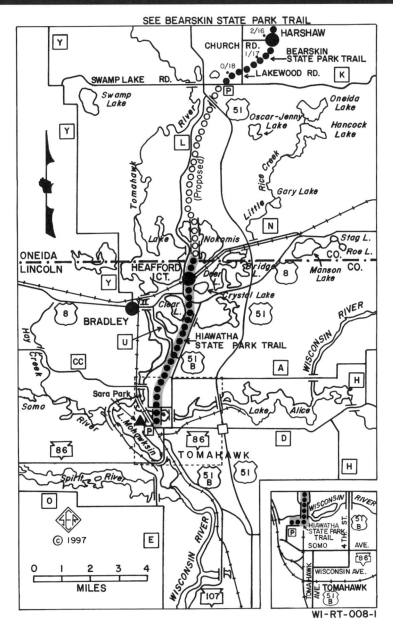

SEE BEARSKIN STATE PARK TRAIL

WI-RT-008-1

HIAWATHA STATE PARK TRAIL
LINCOLN COUNTY
6.6 MILES
SURFACE: SMOOTH CRUSHED GRAVEL

25

BUGLINE RECREATION TRAIL

VICINITY: *Menomonee Falls*
TRAIL LENGTH: *12.2 miles*
SURFACE: *smooth crushed gravel*

TRAIL USE:

(between mile markers 7 & 12)

(between mile markers 1 & 4)

The 12.2-mile Bugline Recreation Trail goes from S.R.-175 in Menomonee Falls to Main Street in Merton, passing through Lannon and Sussex. This trail opened in 1978, and follows the former Chicago, Milwaukee, St. Paul, and Pacific Railroad bed. Horseback riders can enjoy the separate dirt trail that parallels the surfaced trail between "The Ranch" in Menomonee Falls to Menomonee Park, as well as a network of bridle trails in Menomonee Park.

This scenic greenway offers a variety of scenery consisting of wildlife, wetlands, agricultural lands, along with urban and suburban development. Attractions along this trail include "The Ranch" (mile marker 1), the limestone quarries (between mile markers 2 & 3), Menomonee Park (located between mile markers 3 & 4), the Coolings Meadows Nature Preserve (mile marker 6), the Sussex Village Park (located between mile markers 7 & 8), the Town of Lisbon Park (mile marker 11), and Mill Pond (located at mile marker 12).

Future plans for the Bugline Recreation Trail include linking the corridor through Menomonee Falls to the Oak Leaf Trail in Milwaukee.

PARKING:

You'll find parking along streets in Menomonee Falls, Sussex, and Merton. If you're willing to pay a park entrance fee, the parking lot in Menomonee Park is an excellent place to start right next to the trail spur.

FOR MORE INFORMATION:

Waukesha County Parks and Planning Commission
1320 Pewaukee Road
Waukesha, WI 53188
414-548-7790

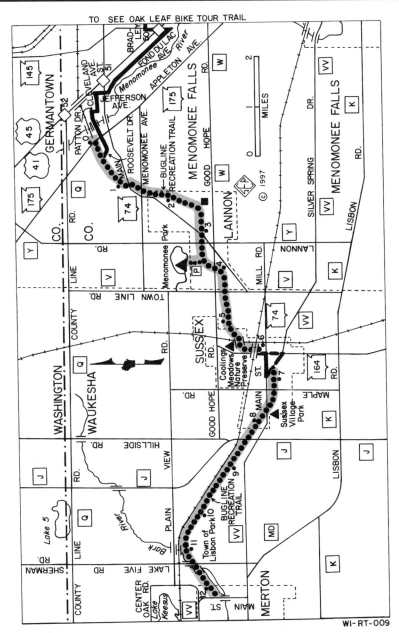

TO SEE OAK LEAF BIKE TOUR TRAIL

BUGLINE RECREATION TRAIL
WAUKESHA COUNTY
12.2 MILES
SURFACE: SMOOTH CRUSHED GRAVEL &
STREETS

WI-RT-009

27

KENOSHA COUNTY BICYCLE TRAIL
VICINITY: *Kenosha*
TRAIL LENGTH: *16.0 miles*
SURFACE: *smooth crushed gravel, asphalt & streets*
TRAIL USE: $\boxed{\$}$ $\boxed{\$}$ $\boxed{\text{🚲}}$ $\boxed{\text{🚴}}$ $\boxed{\text{🚶}}$ $\boxed{\text{⛷}}$ $\boxed{\text{🐎}}$ $\boxed{\text{🛶}}$ $\boxed{\text{🏊}}$ $\boxed{\text{🏍}}$ $\boxed{\text{♿}}$

The 16-mile Kenosha County Bicycle Trail, which opened in 1978, runs in a north-south direction from the Wisconsin-Illinois State Line to the Kenosha-Racine County Line. To the south, the trail continues through Lake County, Illinois, where it is known as the North Shore Bicycle Path. To the north, the trail continues through Racine County, where it is known as the Racine County Bicycle Trail (North Shore Trail).

From the Wisconsin-Illinois State Line, the trail enters Wisconsin with a steel arch bridge crossing over Russel Road. It follows the former Chicago North Shore & Milwaukee Railroad grade to the north for 4 miles, until 89th Street.

The next 8 miles of the bike route follow streets and off road bicycle paths through the city of Kenosha; this 8-mile section of the bike route is known as "The Pike Trail." (The word "Kenosha" is American-Indian for Pike.) A good portion of the Pike Trail follows the Lake Michigan Coast through Kenosha, where it is marked by signs. Attractions along this section of the bike route include Southport Park, the Third Avenue Historic District, Eichelman Park, Wolfenbuttel Park, the Civic Center Historic District, Water Fountain Park, the 1866 Lighthouse, Simmons Island Park, Kennedy Park, and Pennoyer Park. In the north part of Kenosha, you will come to 35th Street, where the Pike Trail ends and the off-road rail-trail starts again.

From 35th Street, the Kenosha County Bicycle Trail goes north another four miles, as it follows the old railroad grade to the Kenosha-Racine County Line. Peorio Park can be visited along this section of the trail. When you reach County Line Road (County Route-KR), you have come to the end of the Kenosha County Bicycle Trail. From this point, you can continue north into Racine County along the Racine County Bicycle Trail (North Shore Trail), or you can turn left onto County Line Road and follow the Racine County 100-mile Bike Route (See address for the Racine County Bicycle Trail).

PARKING:
Parking is available along most city streets in Kenosha and in the city parks along Lake Michigan.

FOR MORE INFORMATION:
Kenosha County Parks
P.O. Box 549, Kenosha, WI 53104-0549
414-857-1862

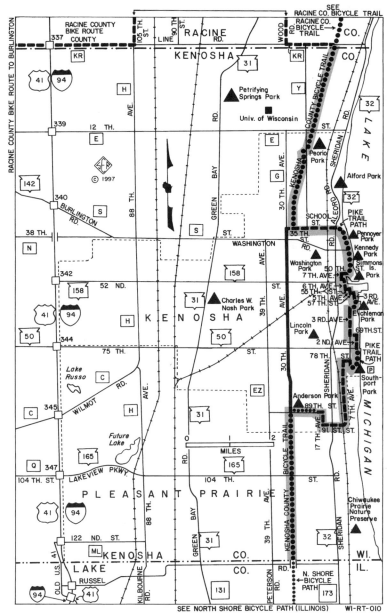

KENOSHA COUNTY BICYCLE TRAIL
KENOSHA COUNTY

16.0 MILES

SURFACE: SMOOTH CRUSHED GRAVEL, ASPHALT, &
STREETS

29

RED CEDAR STATE PARK TRAIL
VICINITY: *Menomonie*
TRAIL LENGTH: *14.5 miles*
SURFACE: *smooth crushed gravel*
TRAIL USE:

The 14.5-mile Red Cedar State Park Trail, which opened in 1981, goes from Menomonie to the Chippewa River, and the Chippewa River State Park Trail. The trail also passes through the towns of Irvington and Downsville. The Red Cedar State Park Trail follows the Red Cedar River for its entire 14.5 miles, giving the trail user many beautiful views of the river bends and rock formations that can be seen all along the trail.

Menomonie is a college town full of beautiful historical buildings. Optional underpasses can be taken under the main roads in Irvington and Downsville to avoid the busy intersections. Between mile markers 8 and 14, you will find yourself in a very wooded area. You will pass through the Dunnville Wildlife Area before crossing the spectacular 800-foot trestle over the Chippewa River. This is also where the 23.5-mile Chippewa River State Park Trail begins, which can be followed all the way to Eau Claire.

PARKING:
Parking is available in Menomonie, Irvington, 370th Avenue, and Downsville.

The 800 foot long trestle crosses over the Chippewa River.

FOR MORE INFORMATION:
Red Cedar State Park Trail
921 Brickyard Rd.,
Menomonie, WI 54751-9100
715-232-1242

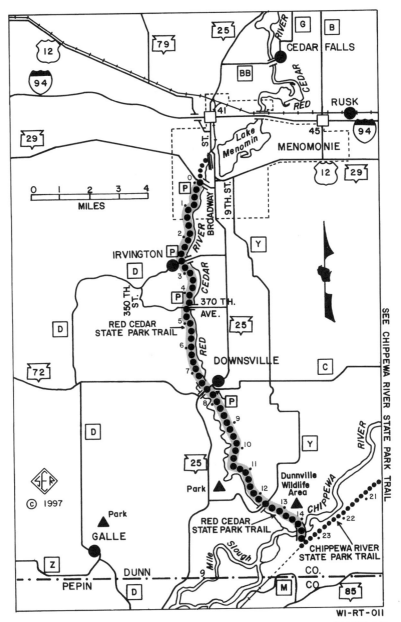

RED CEDAR STATE PARK TRAIL
DUNN COUNTY
14.5 MILES
SURFACE: SMOOTH CRUSHED GRAVEL

WI-RT-0II

31

WIOWASH STATE PARK TRAIL (SOUTH & NORTH)
VICINITY: *Oshkosh/Shawano*
TRAIL LENGTH: *20.3 & 21.0 miles*
SURFACE: *smooth crushed gravel*

TRAIL USE:

The Wiouwash State Park Trail gets its name from the four counties the trail goes through; (WI) Winnebago, (OU) Outagamie, (WA) Waupaca, and (SH) Shawano Counties. During the 1980s and early 1990s, the trail traversed only two counties, and had two different names, the Winnebago County Recreation Trail and the Outagamie County Recreation Trail. In 1996 the Wisconsin Department of Natural Resources decided to manage the two connecting trails, and extended the trail into the Waupaca and Shawano counties. The trail was given one new name, the "Wiouwash" State Park Trail.

The Wiouwash State Park Trail goes by Lake Butte Des Morts.

32

The southern portion of the trail starts near Oshkosh, along West Wind Road, and goes north to Hortonville. Along the way it passes through Allenville, Larson, and Medina. The scenery along this portion of the trail consists mostly of flat farmlands. Some of the attractions include Lake Butte Des Morts, wetlands, native tallgrass preserves, Rat River Crossing, and Black Otter Park/Lake in Hortonville. You must take Lakeview Avenue and Lake Shore Drive to reach Hortonville.

The northern portion of the trail starts near the Waupaca-Shawano County Line and goes north to Aniwa. Along the way it passes through Split Rock, Tigerton, Whittenburg, Eland, and Birnamwood. The scenery consists mostly of gently rolling farmland, with nature and wildlife evident all along the trail. In Eland, the Wiouwash State Park Trail intersects with the 83.4-mile Mountain Bay State Park Trail taking the trail users west to Wausau, and east to Green Bay.

Future plans include linking the northern and southern portions of the Wiouwash State Park Trails together, to make a continuous 85 mile trail.

PARKING:
Parking for the southern portion is abundant in Oshkosh, Allenville, Larsen, Medina, and Hortonville. Parking is still under development for the northern portion, but is available along the streets in most of the villages.

FOR MORE INFORMATION:
OUTAGAMIE COUNTY: Outagamie County Parks
1375 E. Broadway Dr.
Appleton, WI 54915
414-832-4790

SHAWANO COUNTY: Shawano County Planning and Development Dept.
311 N. Main St., Room 3
Shawano, WI 54166
715-526-6766

WAUPACA COUNTY: Waupaca County Parks
811 Harding St.
Waupaca, WI 54981
715-258-6243

WINNEBAGO COUNTY: Winnebago County Department of Parks
500 E. County Road Y
Oshkosh, WI 54901
414-424-0042

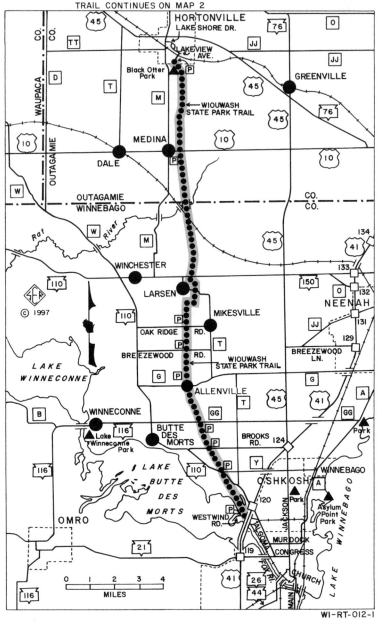

TRAIL CONTINUES ON MAP 2

WI-RT-012-1

WIOUWASH STATE PARK TRAIL (MAP 1)
WINNEBAGO, OUTAGAMIE, WAUPACA, &
SHAWANO COUNTIES
20.3 & 21.0 MILES
SURFACE: SMOOTH CRUSHED GRAVEL

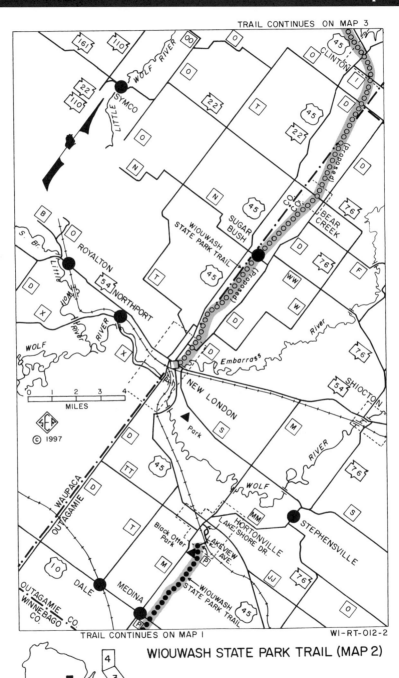

TRAIL CONTINUES ON MAP 3

TRAIL CONTINUES ON MAP 1

WI-RT-012-2

WIOUWASH STATE PARK TRAIL (MAP 2)

© 1997

TRAIL CONTINUES ON MAP 4

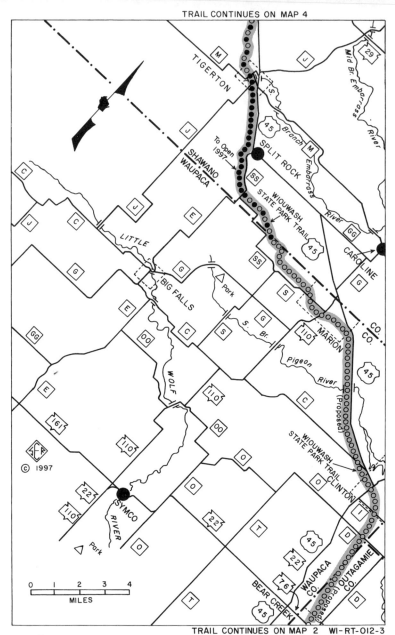

TRAIL CONTINUES ON MAP 2   WI-RT-012-3

WIOUWASH STATE PARK TRAIL (MAP 3)

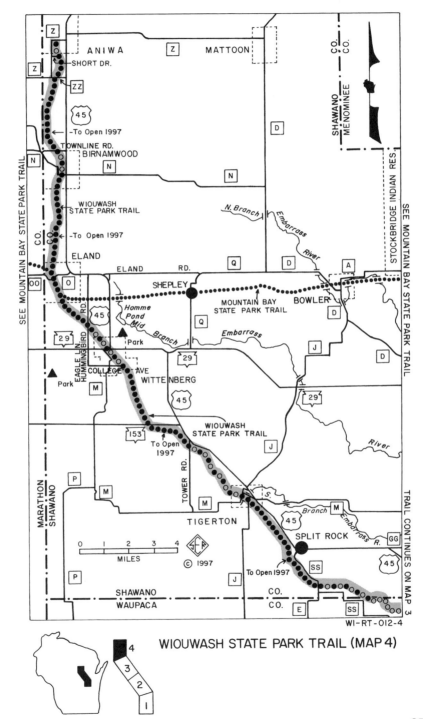

WIOUWASH STATE PARK TRAIL (MAP 4)

WI-RT-012-4

New Berlin Recreation Trail / Waukesha Bike Trails

NEW BERLIN RECREATION TRAIL
VICINITY: *Waukesha*
TRAIL LENGTH: *6.0 miles*
SURFACE: *smooth crushed gravel*
TRAIL USE:

WAUKESHA BIKE TRAILS
VICINITY: *Waukesha*
TRAIL LENGTH: *7.5 miles*
SURFACE: *asphalt, 4.0 miles & City streets, 3.5 miles*
TRAIL USE:

NEW BERLIN RECREATION TRAIL
The six-mile New Berlin Recreation Trail opened in 1984. It follows the Wisconsin Electric Power Co. right-of-way through New Berlin. The east end of the trail (mile marker 0) starts on the Milwaukee-Waukesha County Line (124th Street), and connects to the 94.6-mile Oak Leaf Trail and Greenfield Park in Milwaukee County. A rest stop can be made at Buena Park (between mile markers 2 & 3). From Buena Park, the trail continues west, and ends on Springdale Road (mile marker 6).

PARKING:
Parking is available in Greenfield Park (124th Street in Milwaukee County) and in New Berlin (Springdale Road).

WAUKESHA BIKE TRAILS
The 7.5 mile network of the Waukesha Bike Trails consists of off-road bike paths and signed on-street routes. The Waukesha Bike Trails connect the New Berlin Recreation Trail, and the Glacial Drumlin State Park Trail. A circular signed bike route goes around Waukesha on mostly back streets; a loop bicycle path goes along the Fox River through Downtown Waukesha. Starting in New Berlin on Springdale Road, follow the trail west to Lincoln and Greenfield Avenue (slated to open in 1998). If you want to get through Waukesha quickly, go south on Greenfield Avenue and follow the Southern Loop to College Avenue. From this point, the off-road trail goes one-half mile west, where it becomes the Glacial Drumlin State Park Trail.

PARKING:
Parking for the trail network is on the east end along Springdale Road in New Berlin, and on the west end near College Avenue and Dunbar. Parking is also available along the streets of Waukesha.

FOR MORE INFORMATION:
Waukesha County Parks and Planning Commission
1320 Pewaukee Rd., Waukesha, WI 53188
414-548-7790

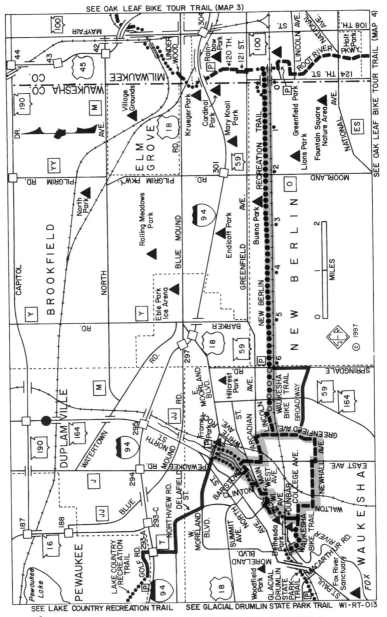

SEE OAK LEAF BIKE TOUR TRAIL (MAP 3)

SEE LAKE COUNTRY RECREATION TRAIL   SEE GLACIAL DRUMLIN STATE PARK TRAIL   WI-RT-013

NEW BERLIN RECREATION TRAIL
WAUKESHA COUNTY
6.0 MILES; SURFACE: SMOOTH CRUSHED GRAVEL

WAUKESHA BIKE TRAILS
WAUKESHA COUNTY
7.5 MILES; SURFACE: ASPHALT(2.5 miles along Fox
River, 1.0 mile on East Side, 0.5 miles on West Side) &
STREETS (3.5 miles).

39

MILITARY RIDGE STATE PARK TRAIL
VICINITY: *Madison/Dodgeville*
TRAIL LENGTH: *38.0 miles*
SURFACE: *smooth crushed gravel*
TRAIL USE: $ 🚌 🚴 🏕 🏃 ⛷ 🐎 🛷 🏊 🏍 ♿

The 38-mile Military Ridge State Park Trail goes from Dodgeville to Verona. Along the way it passes through Ridgeway, Barneveld, Blue Mounds, Mount Horeb, Klevenville, and Riley. The scenery consists of rolling farmland, woods, wetlands, and prairies. The first sections opened in 1985 and this rail-trail follows the former Chicago and North Western Railroad bed.

Towards the western half of the trail you will follow a ridge, where you can enjoy the broad vistas, farmlands, and wooded hillsides. Military Ridge gets its name from the historic 1835 Military Road, where construction was supervised by Colonel Zachary Taylor. The 1835 Military Road was built to link the major lead-mining regions of Southwestern Wisconsin. Near mile marker 2/36 along County Route-Z, an off-road trail spur goes into Governor Dodge State Park. Near mile marker 18/20, another trail spur goes into Blue Mounds State Park. Mounds View Park is at the mid-point of the trail (mile marker 19/19.)

Towards the east half of the trail, the Sugar River Valley consists of glacial moraines, decorated with prairies and wildflowers. A "Cave of the Mounds" tour is available along County Route-F, near mile-marker 20/18. The east end of the Military Ridge State Park Trail is located east of Verona on County Route-PB, at mile marker 38/0. From this point, the Capital City State Trail (slated to open in 1997) leads into Madison, Wisconsin's State Capital. See a description of the Capital City State Trail on page 48.

PARKING:
Parking is available in Dodgeville, Ridgeway, Barneveld, Blue Mounds, Mount Horeb, Riley, Verona, and Highway PD east of Verona.

FOR MORE INFORMATION:
Military Ridge State Park Trail
4175 State Highway 23
Dodgeville, WI 53533-9506
608-935-5119

Shawn E. Richardson bikes the Military Ridge State Park Trail.

A tranquil summer scene along the Military Ridge State Park Trail.

41

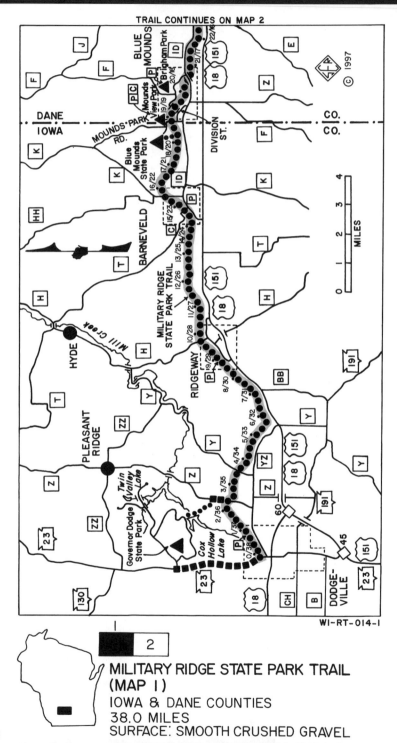

TRAIL CONTINUES ON MAP 2

© 1997

WI-RT-014-1

MILITARY RIDGE STATE PARK TRAIL
(MAP 1)
IOWA & DANE COUNTIES
38.0 MILES
SURFACE: SMOOTH CRUSHED GRAVEL

42

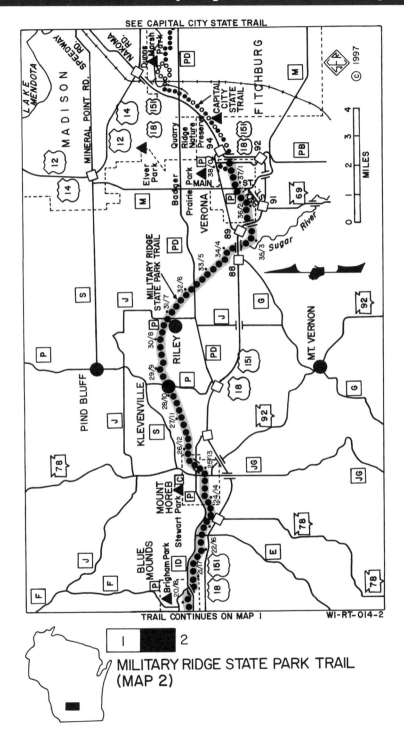

SEE CAPITAL CITY STATE TRAIL

MILITARY RIDGE STATE PARK TRAIL
(MAP 2)

TRAIL CONTINUES ON MAP 1

WI-RT-014-2

© 1997

GLACIAL DRUMLIN STATE PARK TRAIL (WEST & EAST)
VICINITY: *Madison/Waukesha*
TRAIL LENGTH: *21.0 & 28.0 miles. Trail will be 51.0 miles when complete.*
SURFACE: *smooth crushed gravel*

TRAIL USE: 🔞 💲 🚴 🛹 🚶 📷 🐴 ⛷ 🏊 🏍 ♿

The 49-mile Glacial Drumlin State Park Trail runs west to east from Cottage Grove, east of Madison, to Waukesha, west of the Milwaukee area. From the west, the trail goes through Cottage Grove, Deerfield, London, Lake Mills, Jefferson Junction, Helensville, Sullivan, Dousman, Wales, and Waukesha. The trail opened in 1986 and follows the former Chicago and North Western Railroad bed. The trail name comes from the long hills and ridges left behind after the melting of the glaciers, which are called drumlins. Most of the drumlins exist in Jefferson County. The scenery along the trail includes farmland, wetlands, and prairie.

Along the western portion of the trail the highlights include the Deerfield Community Park (mile marker 7), the Mills Wildlife Area (mile marker 14), Rock Lake (between mile markers 14 & 15), the Trail Headquarters in Lake Mills refurbished train station (mile marker 15), the Lake Mills Trail Spur (mile marker 16), and Aztalan State Park (mile marker 18). The trail temporarily ends on the corner of State Route-26 and West Junction Road (mile marker 21). Two miles from here the trail's eastern portion can be reached.

Along the eastern portion of the trail, there is an enjoyable rest stop in Pohmann Park, at mile marker 23. Between the Jefferson-Waukesha County Line and Dousman, mile markers 16 & 13, some huge wetlands give the trail user an opportunity to view all kinds of wildlife. Between Wales and Waukesha, mile markers 6 & 3, the trail winds through some very beautiful hills. In Waukesha, the Glacial Drumlin State Park Trail ends, and the Waukesha Bike Trail begins at mile marker 0, when you cross over the Fox River Bridge into Waukesha.

From the Fox River Bridge you can take the Waukesha Bike Trail and the New Berlin Recreation Trail across eastern Waukesha County into Milwaukee and Milwaukee County, home of the 94.6-mile circular Oak Leaf Trail (see page 10.)

PARKING:
You can find parking in Cottage Grove, Deerfield, London, Lake Mills, Helenville (Switzke Road), Sullivan, Dousman, Wales, and Waukesha.

FOR MORE INFORMATION:

EASTERN PORTION:
Glacial Drumlin State Park Trail
N846 W329/DNR-Lapham,Peak Unit-
KMSF,C.T.H. Co.”C”
Delafield, WI 53018
414-646-3025

WESTERN PORTION:
Glacial Drumlin State Park Trail
Wisconsin Dept. of Natural
Resources, 1213 S. Main St.
Lake Mills, WI 53551-1818
414-648-8774

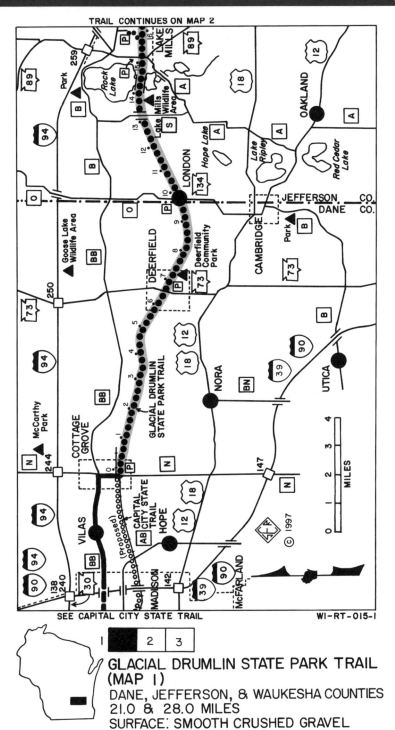

TRAIL CONTINUES ON MAP 2

GLACIAL DRUMLIN STATE PARK TRAIL
(MAP 1)
DANE, JEFFERSON, & WAUKESHA COUNTIES
21.0 & 28.0 MILES
SURFACE: SMOOTH CRUSHED GRAVEL

WI-RT-015-1

SEE CAPITAL CITY STATE TRAIL

45

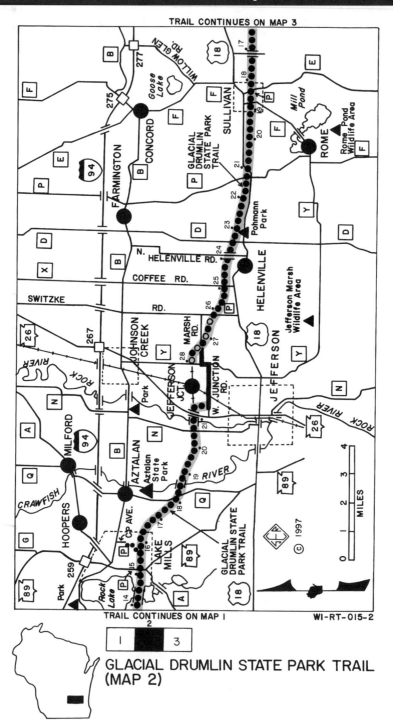

TRAIL CONTINUES ON MAP 3

TRAIL CONTINUES ON MAP I

WI-RT-015-2

GLACIAL DRUMLIN STATE PARK TRAIL
(MAP 2)

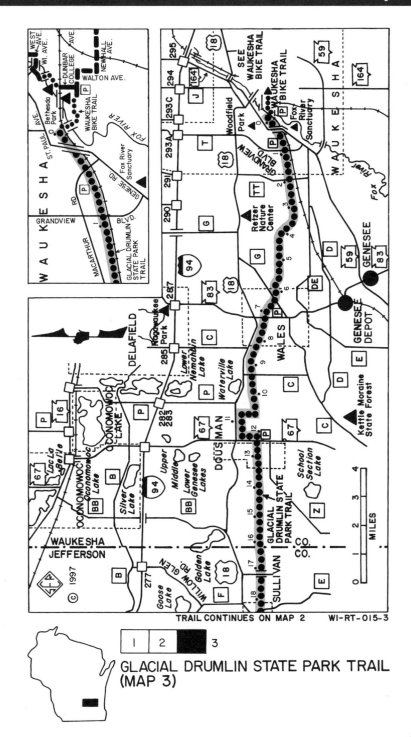

TRAIL CONTINUES ON MAP 2   WI-RT-015-3

GLACIAL DRUMLIN STATE PARK TRAIL
(MAP 3)

47

CAPITAL CITY STATE TRAIL
VICINITY: *Madison*
TRAIL LENGTH: *3.5, 3.0, & 6.5 miles. Entire trail will be 27.0 miles when completed.*
SURFACE: *asphalt*
TRAIL USE:

In 1991, the Capital City State Trail was designed by the City of Madison to create a west-to-east trail corridor that linked both the Military Ridge State Park Trail and the Glacial Drumlin State Park Trail. This 27-mile trail, which is not yet completed, will follow a combination of existing bike paths, open green spaces, and abandoned railroad corridors.

From the West, the first section of the Capital City State Trail starts on the east side of Verona, where the 38-mile Military Ridge State Park Trail ends. The Capital City State Trail follows US Routes-18 & 151 along an abandoned railroad corridor, past the Quarry Ridge Nature Preserve, for 3.5 miles to McKee Road. North of McKee Road, the trail comes out onto a service road. (Scheduled to open in 1997.)

The second section of the Capital City State Trail starts near Dunn's Marsh Park, and goes east for 3.0 miles through a hilly and wooded suburban neighborhood, located between the Seminole Highway and Fish Hatchery Road. (Scheduled to open in 1997.)

The third section of the Capital City State Trail wraps around Lake Monona, and goes for 6.5 miles through the center of Madison. Built in the 1980s, the trail starts on Waunona Way, near the south end of Lake Monona. The trail follows Olin Avenue and John Nolen Drive around Lake Monona to Blair Street. This trail offers spectacular views of Madison's city and capital skyline. You will pass through Olin & Turville Park and Law Park. The trail takes you very close to the State Capital Building and right next to the Convention Center, which was designed by Frank Lloyd Wright. From Blair Street going east, the trail becomes a rail-trail (also known as the Isthmus Bike Path) through the eastern urban neighborhoods of Madison. The trail passes through Olbrich Park and ends on Dempsey Road.

Other sections are expected to be built in the near future. Until then, city streets are the only way to get to the different sections of the Capital City State Trail. To reach the Glacial Drumlin State Park Trail from Dempsey Road, go east on Cottage Grove Road to the town of Cottage Grove. Most of this road has wide paved shoulders. After reaching Cottage Grove, go south on County Route-N to the railroad crossing, where there is parking available for the 49-mile Glacial Drumlin State Park Trail.

PARKING:
Parking is available only at each end of the trail in Verona and Cottage Grove, and along the streets in Madison and Fitchburg.

Madison's city skyline along the Capital City State Trail.

FOR MORE INFORMATION:
Dane County Regional Planning Commission
217 S. Hamilton St., Suite 403
Madison, WI 53703
608-266-4518

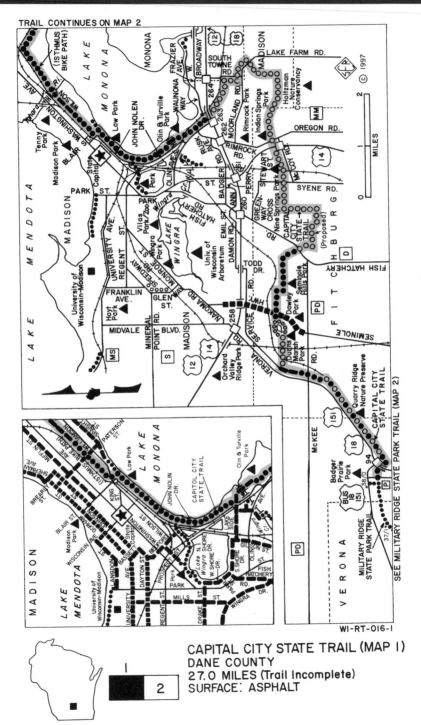

TRAIL CONTINUES ON MAP 2

WI-RT-016-1

CAPITAL CITY STATE TRAIL (MAP 1)
DANE COUNTY
27.0 MILES (Trail Incomplete)
SURFACE: ASPHALT

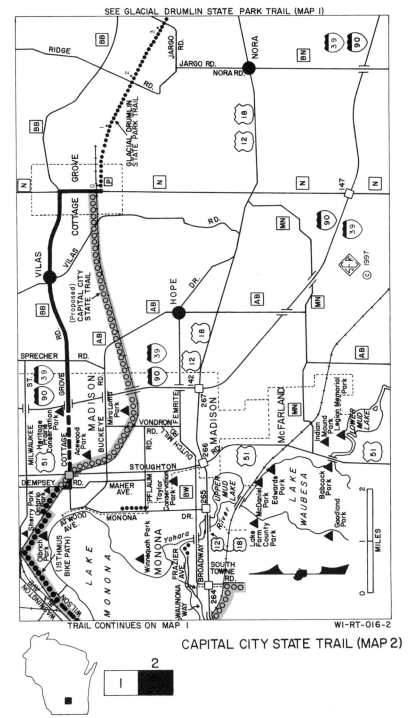

SEE GLACIAL DRUMLIN STATE PARK TRAIL (MAP I)

CAPITAL CITY STATE TRAIL (MAP 2)

WI-RT-016-2

TRAIL CONTINUES ON MAP I

© 1997

51

GREAT RIVER STATE PARK TRAIL
VICINITY: *La Crosse*
TRAIL LENGTH: *24.0 miles*
SURFACE: *smooth crushed gravel*

TRAIL USE: $ 🚻 🚲 🎿 🚶 🔌 🐎 ⛷ ➡ 🏍 ♿

The 24-mile Great River State Park Trail, which opened in 1988, goes from La Crosse to Marshland. It follows the Mississippi River as it winds through Onalaka, Midway, and Trempealeau. The scenery consists of distant bluffs and rock outcrops which can be seen along both sides of the Mississippi River.

The southeast end of the Great River State Park Trail is also the west end of the 21.5-mile La Crosse River State Park Trail in La Crosse. A parking lot is available for both trails along County Route-B, just east of State Route-16. From here, the Great River State Park Trail goes Northwest to Onalaska, where the Visitor's Center is located.

Once you reach the Visitor's Center, there is a small gap in the trail. It is best to go north on Oak Street, which becomes third Avenue. Next, turn left and go west on Irvin Street. After crossing over Second Avenue you can continue north along the off-road Great River State Park Trail.

Highlights along this part of the trail include going through the Upper Mississippi River Wildlife & Fish Refuge, the Trempealeau Wildlife Area, Perrot State Park, and the Trempealeau National Wildlife Refuge. The smooth trail surface ends on West Prairie Road, next to the entrance of the Trempealeau National Wildlife Refuge. The roads and trails are rough between the Trempealeau National Wildlife Refuge and Marshland, so users with standard bicycles and wheelchairs may not want to travel this section of the trail.

PARKING:
You can find parking in La Crosse, Onalaska, Midway, Trempealeau, Trempealeau National Wildlife Refuge, and Marshland.

FOR MORE INFORMATION:
Perrot State Park
P.O. Box 407, Trempealeau, WI 54661
608-534-6409

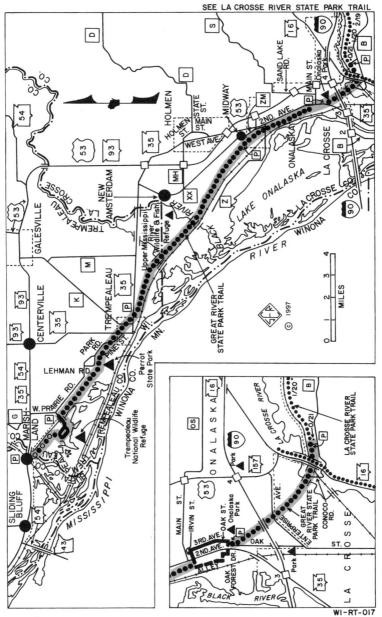

GREAT RIVER STATE PARK TRAIL
LA CROSSE, TREMPEALEAU, & BUFFALO COUNTIES
24.0 MILES
SURFACE: SMOOTH CRUSHED GRAVEL

LA CROSSE RIVER STATE PARK TRAIL

VICINITY: *La Crosse/Sparta*
TRAIL LENGTH: *21.5 miles*
SURFACE: *smooth crushed gravel*
TRAIL USE: 💲 🚳 🚴 ⛸ 🚶 ⛷ 🐴 ⛷ 🏊 🏍 ♿

The 21.5-mile La Crosse River State Park Trail follows the La Crosse River from La Crosse to Sparta. It also passes through West Salem, Bangor, and Rockland. When it opened in 1989, this trail replaced the La Crosse-to-Sparta Section of the former 300-mile Wisconsin Bikeway, which was created back in 1966 and followed mostly backroads from La Crosse to Kenosha and Racine. The La Crosse River State Park Trail follows the former Chicago and North Western Railroad bed, and it also parallels an active railroad. The scenery consists of farmland and wooded hillsides.

The west end of the La Crosse River State Park Trail is also the southeast end of the 24-mile Great River State Park Trail in La Crosse. A parking lot is available for both trails along County Route-B, just east of State Route-16 (mile marker 0/21). The most scenic and tranquil section of the trail is between La Crosse and West Salem. Neshonoc Lake Park is near the trail; however, you must take County Route-C North of West Salem to get to the Lake (mile marker 7/14). Prairie land, including wild-flowers and native grasses, can be seen along the trail from mile markers 11/10 to 15/6. In Sparta, the refurbished train station is the La Crosse River State Park Trail Headquarters (mile marker 21/0). From this spot, the trail goes another half-mile east to John Street. Follow the signs to continue southeast along the 32-mile Elroy-Sparta State Park Trail.

PARKING:

Parking is available in La Crosse, West Salem, Bangor, Rockland, and Sparta.

FOR MORE INFORMATION:
Wildcat Work Unit, P.O. Box 99
Ontario, WI 54651-0099
608-337-4775

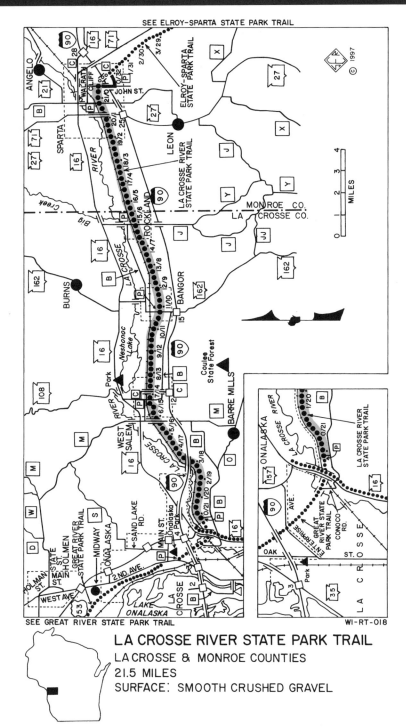

SEE ELROY-SPARTA STATE PARK TRAIL

© 1997

SEE GREAT RIVER STATE PARK TRAIL

WI-RT-018

LA CROSSE RIVER STATE PARK TRAIL
LA CROSSE & MONROE COUNTIES
21.5 MILES
SURFACE: SMOOTH CRUSHED GRAVEL

WILD GOOSE STATE PARK TRAIL
VICINITY: *Fond Du Lac/Juneau*
TRAIL LENGTH: *34.0 miles (some sections incomplete)*
SURFACE: *smooth crushed gravel*
TRAIL USE: $ 🚲 🚶 🐴 🚣 🏍 ♿

🐴 (between mile markers 0/34 to 4/30)

The 34-mile Wild Goose State Park Trail goes south to north from State Route-60, near Clyman, to Fond Du Lac. The trail passes through Juneau, Minnesota Junction, Burnett, Oak Center, and Oakfield. The trail follows the former Chicago North Western Railroad bed. The first sections of the Wild Goose State Park Trail opened to the public in 1989.

The major attractions along the trail include the Horicon National Wildlife Refuge and the Horicon Marsh Wildlife Area, located between mile markers 12/22 & 23/11. The scenery consists mostly of farmland and wooded areas.

PARKING:
Parking is available on State Route-60 near Clyman, the intersection of State Routes-33 & 26 near Minnesota Junction, Market Street in Burnett, State Route-49 on the Dodge-Fond Du Lac County Line, and County Route-VVV in Fond Du Lac.

FOR MORE INFORMATION:
DODGE COUNTY SECTION:
Dodge County Planning & Development Administrative Building, Juneau, WI 53039
414-386-3700

FOND DU LAC SECTION:
Fond Du Lac County Planning & Parks Dept., 160 S. Macy St.
Fond Du Lac, WI 54935-4241
414-929-3135

A rest area along the Wild Goose State Park Trail.

Wild Goose State Park Trail near Waupun, WI.

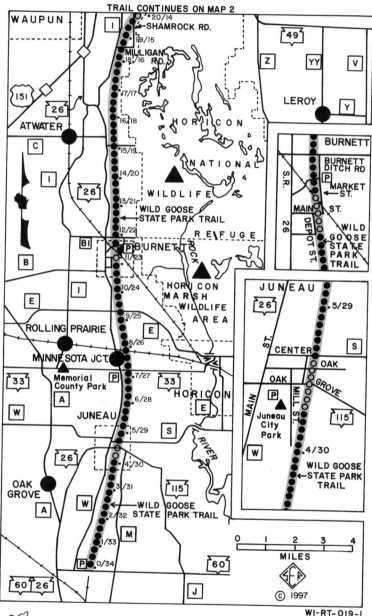

TRAIL CONTINUES ON MAP 2

WAUPUN

20/14
SHAMROCK RD.
19/15
MILLIGAN
18/16 RD.
17/17
16/18
15/19
14/20
13/21
WILD GOOSE
STATE PARK TRAIL
12/22
BURNETT
11/23
10/24
9/25
8/26
7/27
6/28
5/29
4/30
3/31
2/32
1/33
0/34

49

Z   YY   V

LEROY   Y

BURNETT
BURNETT
DITCH RD
MARKET ST.
MAIN   ST.
WILD
GOOSE
STATE
PARK
TRAIL

JUNEAU
5/29
CENTER   S
OAK
OAK   GROVE
115
Juneau
City
Park
W   4/30
WILD GOOSE
STATE PARK
TRAIL

ATWATER
C
I
26
B1
B
I
E
ROLLING PRAIRIE
E
MINNESOTA JCT.
Memorial
County Park   P
33   A   33
W
JUNEAU   E
26   S
OAK
GROVE   W
A   WILD GOOSE
STATE PARK
TRAIL
M
P
60 26   J

151
26

HORICON

NATIONAL

WILDLIFE

REFUGE

HORICON
MARSH
WILDLIFE
AREA

HORICON

RIVER

115

60

S.R. 26
DEPOT ST.
MAIN ST.
MILL ST.
GROVE

0   1   2   3   4
MILES

© 1997

WI-RT-019-1

WILD GOOSE STATE PARK
TRAIL (MAP I)
DODGE & FOND DU LAC COUNTIES
34.0 MILES
SURFACE: SMOOTH CRUSHED
GRAVEL

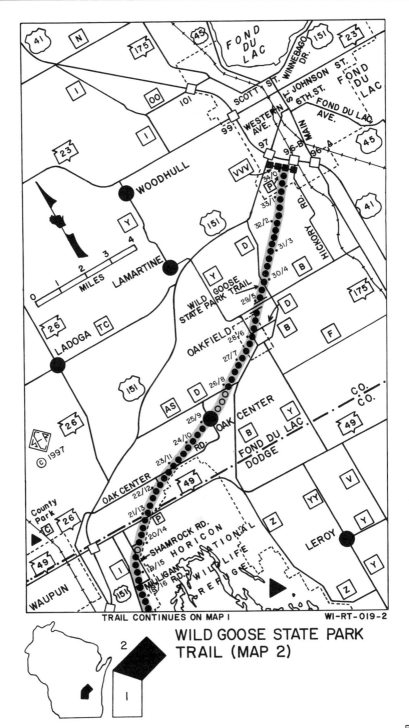

TRAIL CONTINUES ON MAP 1   WI-RT-019-2

WILD GOOSE STATE PARK
TRAIL (MAP 2)

PINE LINE TRAIL
VICINITY: *Medford*
TRAIL LENGTH: *26.2 miles*
SURFACE: *smooth crushed gravel (between mile markers 23 & 26) original ballast (between mile markers 0 & 23)*

TRAIL USE: 💲 💲 🚴 🚵 🏃 🚶 🐎 🎿 ➡️ 🚜 ♿

The 26.2-mile Pine Line gets its name from both the large quantity of pine trees shipped on it between 1870 and 1980, and the beautiful pine trees that still grow along the trail today.

The trail opened in 1990, and runs north to south from Prentice to Medford. Along the way it passes through Ogema, Westboro, Chelsea, and Whittlesey.

The northern half of the trail goes through the terminal moraine formed by the Wisconsin Glacier over 10,000 years ago. The scenery consists of hardwood forested hillsides and cedar wetlands. The southern half of the trail consists of mostly picturesque dairy farms, with a few wooded areas.

The Chequamegon National Forest is located two miles west of the Pine Line Trail (between mile markers 10 & 19). Timms Hill County Park is located four miles east of Ogema (mile marker 5). Attractions along the trail include Chelsea Lake (mile marker 15), and Lions Park (mile marker 22).

Future plans for the Pine Line Trail include giving the rest of the trail a smooth crushed gravel surface, and extending the trail into Prentice and Medford.

PARKING:
Parking is available in Medford along Allman Avenue. You can also park along the streets of Prentice, Ogema, Westboro, Chelsea, and Whittlessey.

FOR MORE INFORMATION:
PRICE COUNTY:
Price County Tourism Office
126 Cherry St.
Phillips, WI 54555
800-269-4505

TAYLOR COUNTY:
Taylor County Tourism Council
224 S. Second St.
Medford, WI 54451
800-257-4729

Dairy farms make up much of the scenery on the Pine Line Trail.

Pine trees along the Pine Line Trail.

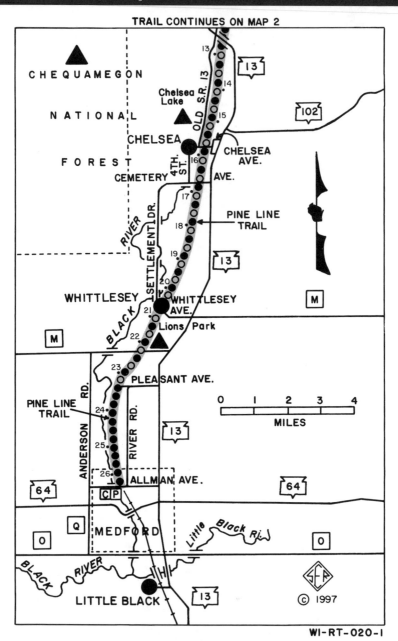

TRAIL CONTINUES ON MAP 2

CHEQUAMEGON

NATIONAL

CHELSEA

FOREST

CEMETERY

Chelsea
Lake

CHELSEA
AVE.

PINE LINE
TRAIL

WHITTLESEY

WHITTLESEY
AVE.

Lions Park

PLEASANT AVE.

PINE LINE
TRAIL

ALLMAN AVE.

MEDFORD

LITTLE BLACK

© 1997

WI-RT-020-1

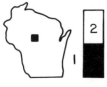

PINE LINE TRAIL (MAP 1)
TAYLOR & PRICE COUNTIES
26.2 MILES
SURFACE: SMOOTH CRUSHED
GRAVEL (between mile markers
23 & 26); the remainder is GRAVEL.

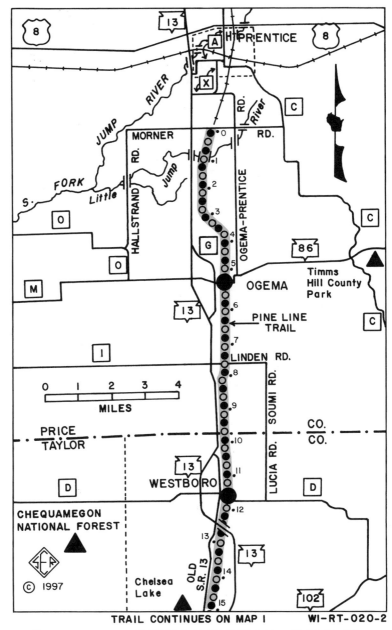

PINE LINE TRAIL (MAP 2)

TRAIL CONTINUES ON MAP 1

WI-RT-020-2

CHEESE COUNTRY RECREATION TRAIL
VICINITY: *Monroe/Mineral Point*
TRAIL LENGTH: *47.0 miles*
SURFACE: *smooth crushed gravel/coarse crushed gravel*

TRAIL USE: 💲 💲 🚴 🏇 🚶 📷 🐎 ⛷ 🏊 🏍 ♿

The 47-mile Cheese Country Recreation Trail opened in 1990. It passes through Iowa, LaFayette, and Green Counties. The trail starts in Mineral Point and heads through Calamine, Darlington, Gratiot, South Wayne, and Browntown to Monroe. The scenery along the trail consists mostly of Wisconsin dairy farms, set among picturesque rolling hill landscapes. The trail also follows a long portion of the Pecatonica River, crossing the river eight times. This trail has a smooth crushed gravel surface, but there are some short sections (mostly through the towns) where the trail has a coarse crushed gravel surface. Even though a standard touring bicycle can be used along the trail with little trouble, a mountain bike would be better suited. This unique trail was also designed to allow a large variety of trail users to enjoy the trail, including ATVs. Mutual respect between all trail users can make the trail much more enjoyable for everyone.

Each bridge along the trail has a two-way directional mile marker number posted on the guardrail's end. Therefore, each bridge, with its unique mile marker location number, is shown on the trail map (e.g. bridge "14.8/0.2").

The Cheese Country Recreation Trail gets its name from the 30 cheese factories in Iowa, LaFayette, and Green Counties. From the northwest end, the trail starts on Old Darlington Road, in Mineral Point. The town is known for its mining history, and the many nostalgic shops, antique shops, and tourist attractions that exist there today. Going south along the trail, the next village is Calamine. This is where the Cheese Country Recreation Trail intersects the 10-mile Pecatonica State Park Trail (just south of County Route G).

From Calamine, the Cheese Country Recreation Trail follows the Pecatonica River southeast to Darlington. Darlington is the county seat of LaFayette County, with a very beautiful courthouse. The old Darlington Depot is a museum preserving the history of the railbed the recreational trail now follows.

From Darlington, the trail continues to wind its way southeast to Gratiot, then east to South Wayne and Browntown. This portion of the recreation trail also follows the Pecatonica River very closely. The trail goes through a spectacular wetland between Darlington and Gratiot, near bridge 4.1/6.4. In Browntown, the trail is adjacent to the Browntown-Cadiz Springs Recreation Area.

From Browntown, the trail continues east towards Monroe. Here, you will find a memorial rest area and shelter, built in memory of Bill Cowell, a local snowmobiler accidentally killed by a motorist. A scenic crossing over Honey Creek to Monroe brings the trail to its end along Twenty-first Street.

PARKING:

Parking is available in Mineral Point, Calamine, Darlington, Gratiot, South Wayne, Browntown, and Monroe.

A railroad museum is located inside Darlington's Depot.

Railroad memories, Darlington, WI.

FOR MORE INFORMATION:

Tri-County Trail Commission
627 Washington St.
Darlington, WI 53530
608-776-4830

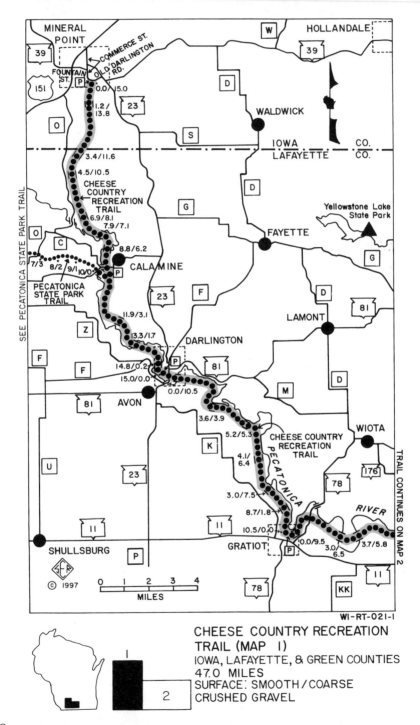

CHEESE COUNTRY RECREATION
TRAIL (MAP I)
IOWA, LAFAYETTE, & GREEN COUNTIES
47.0 MILES
SURFACE: SMOOTH / COARSE
CRUSHED GRAVEL

WI-RT-021-1

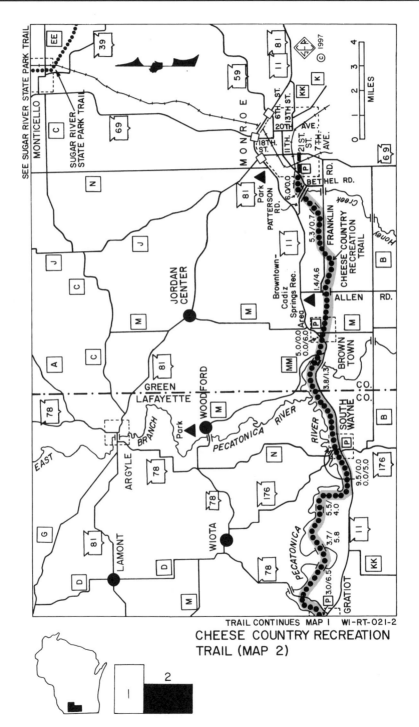

CHEESE COUNTRY RECREATION
TRAIL (MAP 2)

TRAIL CONTINUES MAP I   WI-RT-021-2

OMAHA TRAIL
VICINITY: *Elroy*
TRAIL LENGTH: *12.5 Miles*
SURFACE: *coarse asphalt*
TRAIL USE: 💲 💲 🚴 🚵 🏃 📷 🐴 ⛷️ 🛷 🚜 ♿

The 12.5-mile Omaha Trail opened in 1992. It follows the former Chicago and North Western Railroad bed from Elroy, through Hustler, to Camp Douglas. This trail is a County Trail and not a State Park Trail, so a separate trail fee is required for trail use. The scenery along the Omaha Trail consists of rolling farmland, rock bluffs, and plenty of wooded areas.

From the south, the Omaha Trail starts in Elroy, where both the 32-mile Elroy-Sparta State Park Trail and the 22-mile 400 State Park Trail come together. From Elroy, go north on Academy Street, east on Crandon Street, then north on Second Street. This is where the off-road trail begins (mile marker 0/12).

Going north, you will cross over State Route 80/82. Between mile markers 1/11 and 5/7, you will gradually climb a long, gentle grade towards the highest point of the trail. Once you're there you will go through an old 875-foot railroad tunnel (located between mile markers 5/7 & 6/6). A rest area, with restrooms, is on the north end of the tunnel. You may want to bring a flashlight and jacket along when you go through the tunnel. Between mile markers 6/6 and 9/3, you will coast down a gentle grade on the other side of the "big hill" to Hustler. Between Hustler and Camp Douglas, the Omaha Trail is relatively flat. Despite the trail's flatness, scenic bluffs are visible along this stretch of the trail. The trail ends on County Route-H in the town of Camp Douglas, which has both Army and Air National Guard installations just north of I-90 & 94.

PARKING:
Parking is available in Elroy, Hustler, and Camp Douglas.

FOR MORE INFORMATION:
Dale Dorow, Administrator
250 Oak St, Mauston, WI 53948
608-847-9389

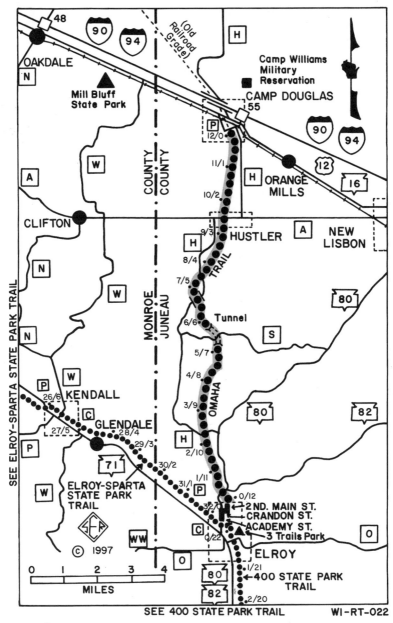

OMAHA TRAIL
JUNEAU COUNTY
12.5 MILES
SURFACE: COARSE ASPHALT

CHIPPEWA RIVER STATE PARK TRAIL

VICINITY: *Eau Claire*

TRAIL LENGTH: *23.5 miles*

SURFACE: *asphalt (0-7 mile markers), coarse asphalt (7-23 mile markers)*

TRAIL USE:

The 23.5-mile Chippewa River State Park Trail follows the Chippewa River from Eau Claire to the south end of the 14.5-mile Red Cedar State Park Trail. The first section of the trail opened in 1992.

The east entrance of the Chippewa River State Park Trail starts in Downtown Eau Claire. There is no trail fee for the trail between mile markers 0 & 5. A steel railroad trestle crosses over the Chippewa River, just north of Grand Avenue, at mile marker 0. The trail goes south, then west, through some of Eau Claire's older neighborhoods. Along the north bank of the Chippewa River, you'll see bluffs and rock outcrops. The trail crosses over to the south bank of the Chippewa River at the western end of Eau Claire, then continues west. Parking is available near Jopke Road, outside Eau Claire.

From this parking spot to the west, a trail fee is required for the Chippewa River State Park Trail (between mile markers 5 & 23).

From Jopke Road to the west, the trail winds along the wooded bank of the Chippewa River. Near mile-marker 7, there is a rest area with a view of the Chippewa River. Rollerbladers may want to turn around at this point, since this is where the smooth asphalt becomes a coarse asphalt trail. From the rest area to Careyville, the trail goes through an open area of flat fields. There is a grocery store in Careyville, if you need a break. Going west from Careyville (between mile markers 13 & 15), you'll see a bend in the Chippewa River. Most of the scenery between Careyville and the quiet village of Meridean consists of thick wooded areas. From Meridean to the west end of the Chippewa River State Park Trail (between mile markers 19 & 23), these wooded areas co-exist with plenty of wetlands, giving the trail user the feeling of being very close to nature. The trail makes a sharp curve to cross an 800-foot trestle over the Chippewa River to the south entrance of the 14.5-mile Red Cedar State Park Trail.

PARKING:

Parking is available in Eau Claire, at the rest area along State Route-85, and on city streets in Careyville.

FOR MORE INFORMATION:

Wisconsin DNR, Western Division
1300 W. Clairmont Ave., P.O. Box 4001
Eau Claire, WI 54701-6127
715-839-1607

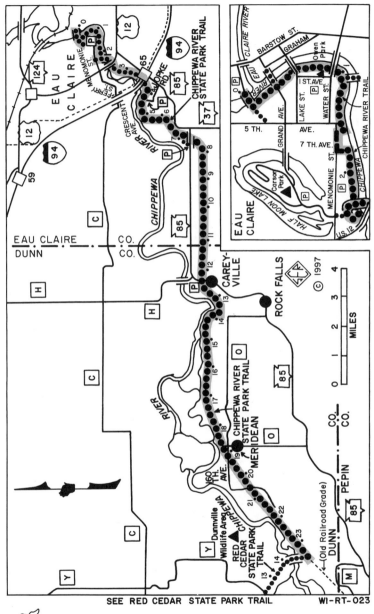

SEE RED CEDAR STATE PARK TRAIL   WI-RT-023

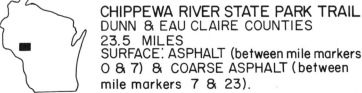

CHIPPEWA RIVER STATE PARK TRAIL
DUNN & EAU CLAIRE COUNTIES
23.5 MILES
SURFACE: ASPHALT (between mile markers
0 & 7) & COARSE ASPHALT (between
mile markers 7 & 23).

400 STATE PARK TRAIL
VICINITY: *Elroy/Reedsburg*
TRAIL LENGTH: *22.0 miles*
SURFACE: *smooth crushed gravel*
TRAIL USE:

HILLSBORO STATE PARK TRAIL
VICINITY: *Hillsboro*
TRAIL LENGTH: *4.3 miles*
SURFACE: *smooth crushed gravel*
TRAIL USE:

The 22-mile 400 State Park Trail follows the Chicago & North Western Railroad bed from Elroy to Reedsburg. Along the way it passes through Union Center, Wonewoc, and La Valle. The "400" was named for the passenger train which took 400 minutes to travel the 400 miles between Chicago, Illinois and Minneapolis/St. Paul, Minnesota. This trail opened in 1993, and replaced the Elroy to Reedsburg Section of the former 300-mile Wisconsin Bikeway.

The scenery along the trail includes wetlands, sandstone bluffs, rolling pastures, farmlands, and eight crossings of the Baraboo River. In Elroy, the 400 State Park Trail intersects with the 32-mile Elroy-Sparta State Park Trail and the 12-mile Omaha Trail, which requires a separate trail fee. In Union Center, between mile markers 4/18 & 5/17, you can take the 4.3-mile Hillsboro State Park Trail west

Bluffs are visible along the 400 State Park Trail.

to Hillsboro. Other attractions include the Hemlock County Park (mile marker 14/8), Lake Redstone County Park (mile marker 16/6), and the Reedsburg Depot, which is now the 400 State Park Trail's visitor's center (mile marker 22/0).

PARKING:
Parking is available in Elroy, Union Center, Hillsboro, Wonewoc, La Valle, and Reedsburg.

FOR MORE INFORMATION:
Wildcat Work Unit, P.O. Box 99
Ontario, WI 54651-0099
608-337-4775

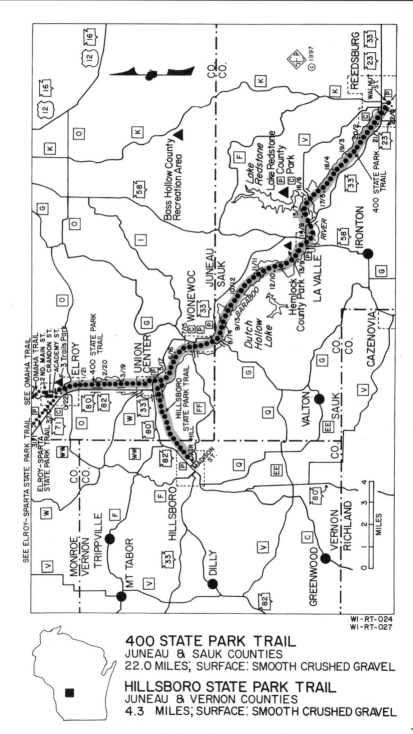

WI-RT-024
WI-RT-027

400 STATE PARK TRAIL
JUNEAU & SAUK COUNTIES
22.0 MILES; SURFACE: SMOOTH CRUSHED GRAVEL

HILLSBORO STATE PARK TRAIL
JUNEAU & VERNON COUNTIES
4.3 MILES; SURFACE: SMOOTH CRUSHED GRAVEL

73

TRI-COUNTY RECREATION CORRIDOR TRAIL

VICINITY: *Superior/Ashland*
TRAIL LENGTH: *61.8 miles*
SURFACE: *smooth crushed gravel & asphalt*
TRAIL USE: 💲 💲 🚲 🚵 🚶 ⛷ 🐎 🏄 ➡ 🛵 ♿

OSAUGIE TRAIL

VICINITY: *Superior*
TRAIL LENGTH: *5.0 miles; will be 8.7 miles when complete*
SURFACE: *asphalt*
TRAIL USE: 💲 💲 🚲 🚵 🚶 ⛷ 🐎 🏄 ➡ 🛵 ♿

The Tri-County Recreation Corridor Trail goes through Douglas, Bayfield, and Ashland Counties. The Osaugie Trail goes from Superior to Ashland and passes through Wentworth, Maple, Blueberry, Bellwood, Brule, Iron River, Ino, and Moquah, roughly following US Route-2 through Northern Wisconsin.

In Superior, the trail is known as the Osaugie Trail and consists of an asphalt surface. Most of the trail was built in 1994. You can start the trail near the corner of Second Street and Second Avenue. There is a tourist information center with an enjoyable view of Lake Superior. The trail goes two miles northwest to Connors Point (slated to open in 1998). To the southeast, the Osaugie Trail follows Second Street and the Lake Superior coast for 2.5 miles to 30th Avenue, where you'll find parking. The Tri-County Recreation Corridor Trail starts at this point, and goes another 2.5 miles southeast as an asphalt trail to Moccasin Mike Road. From here, a four-mile bike path is planned to semi-circle the Allouez Bay.

The Tri-County Trail leaves the city of Superior to the southeast from Moccasin Mike Road. This is where the smooth crushed gravel trail surface begins (scheduled to be surfaced in 1997) between Superior and Ashland. The trail follows the former Northern Pacific Railroad bed.

This trail is definitely a wilderness experience, offering views of Wisconsin's north woods and wildlife. Attractions in Douglas County include Amnicon Falls State Park and the Brule River State Forest. In Bayfield County, you will travel through the Chequamegon National Forest. In Ashland County, the trail goes for 1.5 miles to the city of Ashland on State Route-112.

When riding this trail, be sure to be prepared! You may want to consider that much of this trail goes through some very remote areas, so make sure your bicycle and traveling equipment are in top shape. Remember, this trail includes a wide variety of users, including ATVs. Mutual respect for other trail users will make the trail trip more enjoyable for everyone.

PARKING:
Parking lots are available in Superior along Second Street, on Second Avenue, and on 30th Avenue. You'll also find parking in Brule, Iron River, and Ashland.

A boatyard near the Osaugie Trail.

A bicyclist on the Tri-County Recreation Trail.

FOR MORE INFORMATION:

TRI COUNTY RECREATION
CORRIDOR TRAIL:
Richard Mackey
P.O. Box 503
Ashland, WI 54806
715-682-5299

OSAUGIE TRAIL:
Superior Parks & Recreation
1407 Hammond Ave.
Superior, WI 54880
715-394-0270

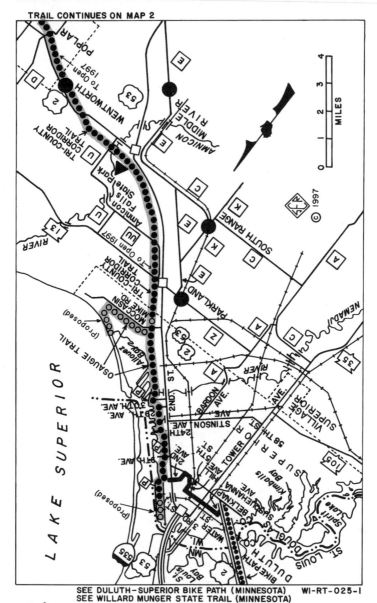

TRAIL CONTINUES ON MAP 2

SEE DULUTH-SUPERIOR BIKE PATH (MINNESOTA)   WI-RT-025-I
SEE WILLARD MUNGER STATE TRAIL (MINNESOTA)

TRI-COUNTY CORRIDOR TRAIL (MAP I)
DOUGLAS, BAYFIELD, & ASHLAND COUNTIES
61.8 MILES
SURFACE: SMOOTH CRUSHED GRAVEL &
ASPHALT

OSAUGIE TRAIL
DOUGLAS COUNTY
2.7 MILES; SURFACE: ASPHALT

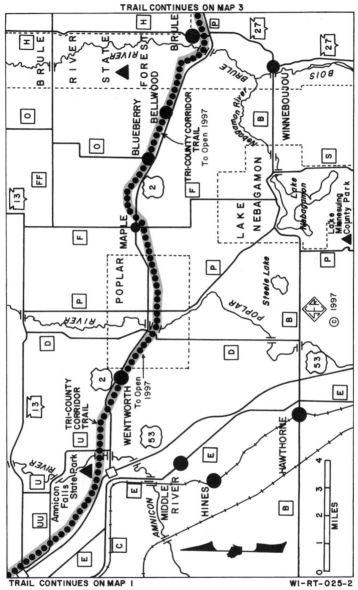

TRAIL CONTINUES ON MAP 3

TRAIL CONTINUES ON MAP I

WI-RT-025-2

TRI-COUNTY CORRIDOR TRAIL (MAP 2)

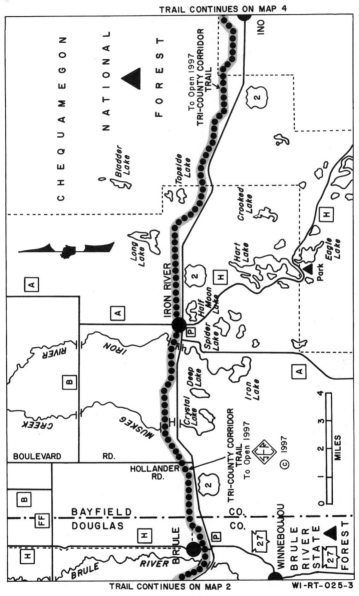

TRAIL CONTINUES ON MAP 4

TRAIL CONTINUES ON MAP 2

WI-RT-025-3

TRI-COUNTY CORRIDOR TRAIL (MAP 3)

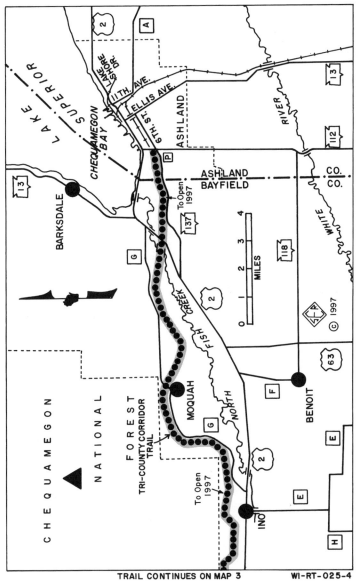

TRAIL CONTINUES ON MAP 3   WI-RT-025-4

TRI-COUNTY CORRIDOR TRAIL (MAP 4)

79

LAKE COUNTRY RECREATION TRAIL
VICINITY: *Waukesha*
TRAIL LENGTH: *8.0 miles*
SURFACE: *asphalt, smooth crushed gravel, and some asphalt streets.*
TRAIL USE: 🛈 🛈 🚲 🛷 🚶 ⛷ 🐎 🛷 🏊 🏍 ♿

The Lake Country Recreation Trail follows the former Milwaukee-Watertown Interurban Railway. In the late 1800s, passengers traveled this very popular line between Waukesha and the Oconomowoc Lake Country. In 1994, almost a century later, this trail opened to a new form of recreation.

The Lake Country Recreation Trail starts north of Waukesha along Golf Club Road near County Route-T. The Landsberg Center Trail parking and rest area is located here. From there, the trail goes west to Delafield. Highlights along the way include West Park, Pewaukee Lake, Nagawaukee Park, Firemans Park, Lake Nagauica, Cushing Park, and Upper Nemahbin Lake. Future plans include extending the trail in both directions.

PARKING:
You'll find parking along Golf Club Road near County Route-T, Nagawaukee Park, near Hartland Road (State Route-83), and Wells Street in Delafield.

The view of Pewaukee Lake along the Lake Country Recreation Trail.

FOR MORE INFORMATION:
Waukesha County Parks & Planning Commission
1320 Pewaukee Rd., Waukesha, WI 53188
414-548-7790

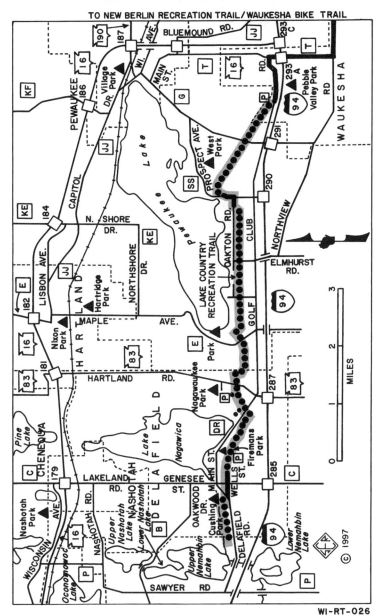

WI-RT-026

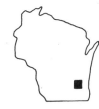

LAKE COUNTRY RECREATION TRAIL
WAUKESHA COUNTY
8.0 MILES
SURFACE: SMOOTH CRUSHED GRAVEL,
ASPHALT, & STREETS

GANDY DANCER STATE PARK TRAIL

VICINITY: *Superior/St. Croix Falls*

TRAIL LENGTH: *91.0 miles*

SURFACE: *smooth crushed gravel for 48.0 miles through Burnett & Polk Counties, the remaining 43.0 miles is original ballast*

TRAIL USE *for Burnett & Polk Counties*:

TRAIL USE *for Douglas County*:

TRAIL USE *for the State of Minnesota*:

The Gandy Dancer State Park Trail opened in 1995, and follows the abandoned Soo Line railbed. A 48-mile smooth crushed gravel trail has been developed from St.Croix Falls to Danbury, Wisconsin, through both Polk and Burnett Counties. Along the way, the trail passes through Centuria, Milltown, Luck, Frederic, Lewis, Siren, Webster, and Oakland. You'll find scenic river crossings over Straight River, Wood River, Clam River, Yellow River (two crossings), and the St. Croix River.

The undeveloped 43.0 miles through Douglas County and the State of Minnesota consists of a very rough gravel surface. Eventually this section may be developed, giving the trail users a 91-mile trail from St. Croix Falls to Superior.

PARKING:

Parking is available in Luck, Siren, and Danbury. You'll also find parking along city streets in St. Croix Falls, Centuria, Milltown, Frederic, Lewis, Webster, and Oakland.

FOR MORE INFORMATION:

BURNETT COUNTY SECTION:
Burnett County Forest and Parks Department
7410 County Highway K, Siren, WI 54872-0106
715-349-2157

DOUGLAS COUNTY SECTION:
Douglas County Forestry Department
P.O. Box 211, Solon Springs, WI 54873
715-378-2219

POLK COUNTY SECTION:
Polk County Information Center
710 Highway 35 South, St. Croix Falls, WI 54024
800-222-7655

STATE OF MINNESOTA SECTION:
Minnesota DNR, Trails and Waterways Unit
Route 2, 701, S. Kenwood
Moose Lake, MN 55767
218-485-5410

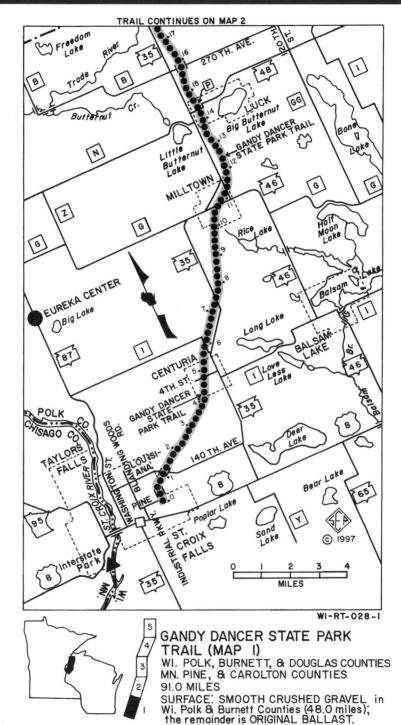

TRAIL CONTINUES ON MAP 2

GANDY DANCER STATE PARK TRAIL

WI-RT-028-1

GANDY DANCER STATE PARK TRAIL (MAP I)

WI. POLK, BURNETT, & DOUGLAS COUNTIES
MN. PINE, & CAROLTON COUNTIES
91.0 MILES
SURFACE: SMOOTH CRUSHED GRAVEL in
Wi. Polk & Burnett Counties (48.0 miles);
the remainder is ORIGINAL BALLAST.

83

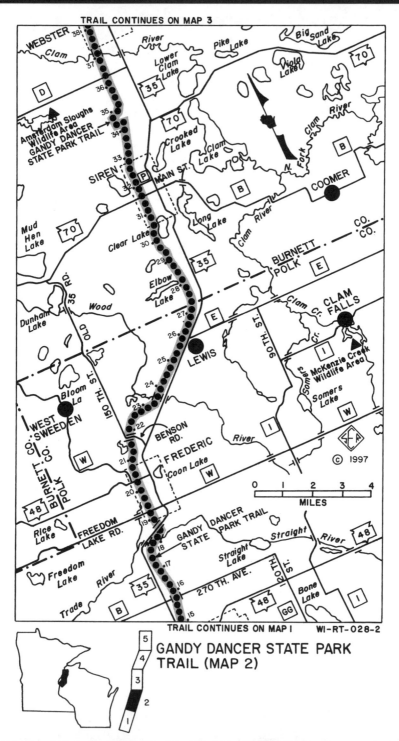

TRAIL CONTINUES ON MAP 3

GANDY DANCER STATE PARK
TRAIL (MAP 2)

WI-RT-028-2

TRAIL CONTINUES ON MAP 1

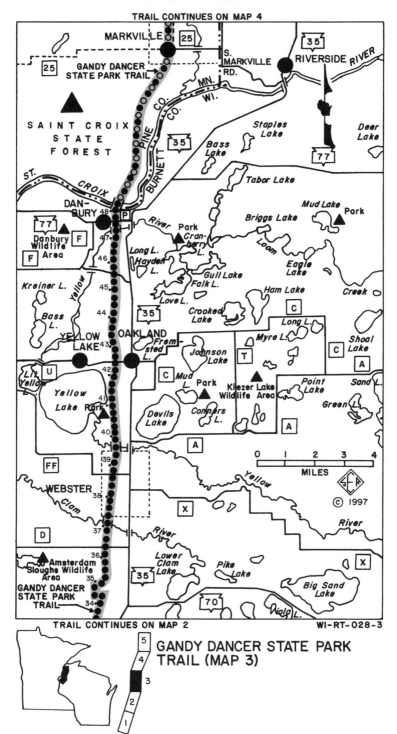

TRAIL CONTINUES ON MAP 4

GANDY DANCER STATE PARK TRAIL (MAP 3)

WI-RT-028-3

85

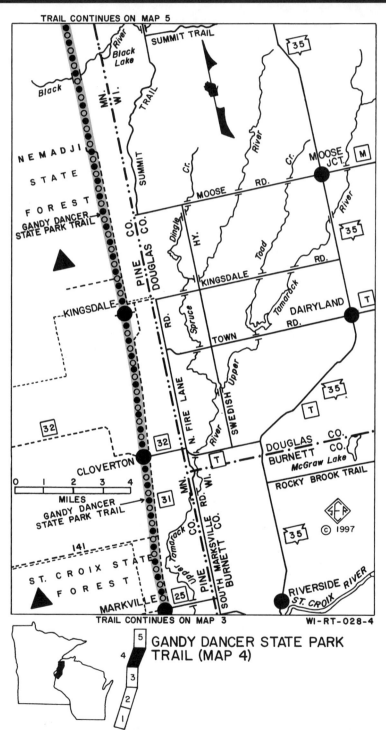

TRAIL CONTINUES ON MAP 5

SUMMIT TRAIL

35

River
Black
Lake

Black

NEMADJI

STATE

FOREST

GANDY DANCER
STATE PARK TRAIL

MN. / WI.

SUMMIT TRAIL

MOOSE RD.

MOOSE
JCT.

M

MOOSE

HY.

Cr.

River

Cr.

Dingle

Toad

River

35

PINE CO. / DOUGLAS CO.

KINGSDALE

RD.

KINGSDALE

Spruce

River

DAIRYLAND

Tamarack

RD.

T

TOWN

RD.

SWEDISH Upper

N. FIRE LANE

32

32

T

35

T

CLOVERTON

DOUGLAS CO.
BURNETT CO.

McGraw Lake

ROCKY BROOK TRAIL

0 1 2 3 4
MILES

GANDY DANCER
STATE PARK TRAIL

31

MN. / WI.

RD.

PINE CO. / MARKSVILLE CO.

SOUTH MARKSVILLE CO.

Upper Tamarack

35

©1997

141

ST. CROIX STATE

FOREST

MARKVILLE

25

RIVERSIDE RIVER

ST. CROIX

TRAIL CONTINUES ON MAP 3

WI-RT-028-4

5
4
3
2
1

**GANDY DANCER STATE PARK
TRAIL (MAP 4)**

86

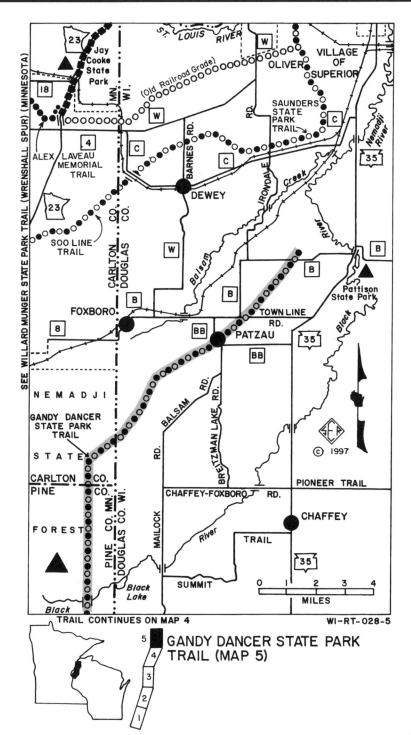

GANDY DANCER STATE PARK
TRAIL (MAP 5)

ROCK TRAIL / SPRING BROOK TRAIL
VICINITY: *Janesville*
TRAIL LENGTH: *6.0 miles*
SURFACE: *asphalt & asphalt streets*

TRAIL USE:

The six-mile Rock Trail and Spring Brook Trail follows the Rock River and the Spring Brook in an east-west direction, through the city of Janesville. Janesville, a community rich in culture and heritage, was named after the early settler Henry Janes, following the Blackhawk War of 1832. The first sections of this trail opened in 1995.

The Rock Trail starts near Afton Road (County Route-D) and follows streets through the older neighborhoods of Janesville for several blocks, until reaching Riverside Street. The bike route becomes off-road here, and the Rock Trail goes through Monterey Park, following the Rock River to Franklin Street. From here, the rail-trail section of the Rock Trail takes you south across a trestle to Delevan Drive (County Route-O). Before reaching Delevan Drive, you can follow the Spring Brook Trail through Jeffris Park, Lions Park, Blackhawk Park, and Palmer Park through the eastern neighborhoods of Janesville.

PARKING:
You'll find parking for the Janesville's Rock/Spring Brook Trails in most of Janesville's city parks.

Cyclists and joggers enjoy the trails in Janesville.

FOR MORE INFORMATION:
City of Janesville, Leisure Services Division
17 N. Franklin St.
Janesville, WI 53545
608-755-3025

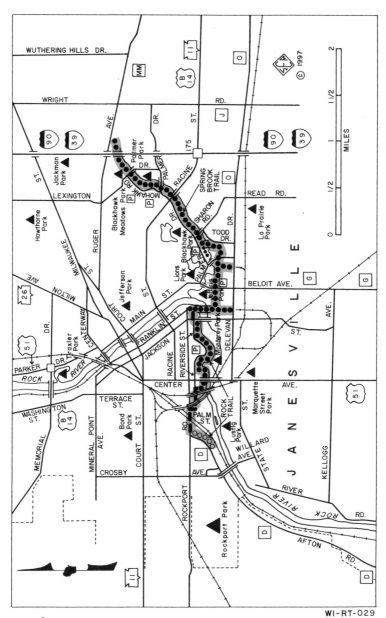

WI-RT-029

ROCK/SPRINGBROOK TRAILS
ROCK COUNTY
6.0 MILES
SURFACE: ASPHALT & STREETS

GLACIAL RIVER TRAIL

VICINITY: *Fort Atkinson*
TRAIL LENGTH: *4.0 Miles*
SURFACE: *asphalt & smooth crushed gravel & city streets*
TRAIL USE: $ ⑤ 🚲 🛴 🚶 ⛷ 🐎 ⛷ 🚧 🚲 ♿

The 4-mile Glacial River Trail follows the former Chicago and North Western Railroad bed from Fort Atkinson to Koshkonong Lake Road near Lake Koshkonong. The Trail opened in 1996.

A parking lot is located along Farmco Lane and Janesville Avenue in Fort Atkinson. From there, the Fort Atkinson-Koshkonong Recreation Trail goes south. The trail crosses Allen Creek, then comes out on Groeler Road. From here, the route follows roads for a short distance, to get around the State Route-26 and Janesville Avenue Interchange. From Schwemmer Lane, the off-road trail picks up again, and wraps around the interchange. There are some great views of Wisconsin's rolling farmland here. The trail continues between State Route-26 and Old 26 Road to Koshkonong Lake Road. Future plans include extending the trail in both directions to Janesvilles and the Glacial Drumlin State Park Trail.

PARKING:

Parking is available in Fort Atkinson, near the corner of Farmco Lane and Janesville Avenue.

Gently rolling farmland is visible from the Glacial River Trail.

FOR MORE INFORMATION:

Jefferson County Parks Department Courthouse
320 South Main Street, Jefferson, WI 53549
414-674-7260

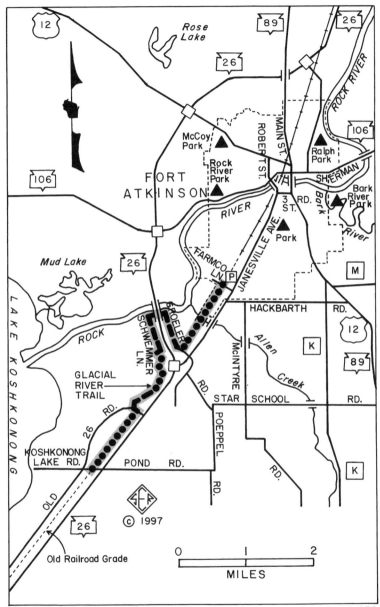

WI-RT-030

GLACIAL RIVER TRAIL
JEFFERSON COUNTY
4.0 MILES
SURFACE: ASPHALT, SMOOTH
CRUSHED GRAVEL, & STREETS

91

MOUNTAIN-BAY STATE PARK TRAIL

VICINITY: *Green Bay/Wausau*
TRAIL LENGTH: *83.4 miles*
SURFACE: *smooth crushed gravel*
TRAIL USE:

The 83.4-mile Mountain-Bay State Park Trail follows the former Chicago and North Western Railroad bed through northeastern Wisconsin, from Wausau to Green Bay. The trail opened in 1995, and goes from west to east through Marathon, Shawano, and Brown Counties. From Kelly (near Wausau), the trail passes through Callon, Ringle, Hatley, Norrie, Eland, Shepley, Bowler, Lyndhurst, Thornton, Shawano, Bonduel, Zachow, Pulaski, Kunesh, Anston, and Howard (near Green Bay). The scenery along the trail consists mostly of gently rolling farmland and wooded areas.

The Mountain-Bay State Park Trail intersects with the 21-mile Wiouwash State Park Trail (Northern Portion) in Eland (Shawano County). To the north, you can go as far as Aniwa; to the south, you can go as far as Split Rock.

PARKING:

In Marathon County, parking can be found in Kelly, Ringle, Hatley, and Norrie. In Brown County, you can find parking in Pulaski, Kunesh, Anston, and Howard. In Shawano County, parking lots have not been established. Parking can be found, however, along most streets in Eland, Shepley, Bowler, Lyndhurst, Thornton, Shawano, Bonduel, and Zachow.

FOR MORE INFORMATION:

BROWN COUNTY:
Brown County Park Department
305 E. Walnut, P.O. Box 23600
Green Bay, WI 54305-3600
414-448-4466

MARATHON COUNTY:
Marathon County Park Department
500 Forest, Wausau, WI 54403
715-847-5235

SHAWANO COUNTY:
Shawano County Planning Dept.
311 N. Main St., Shawano, WI 54166
715-524-5165

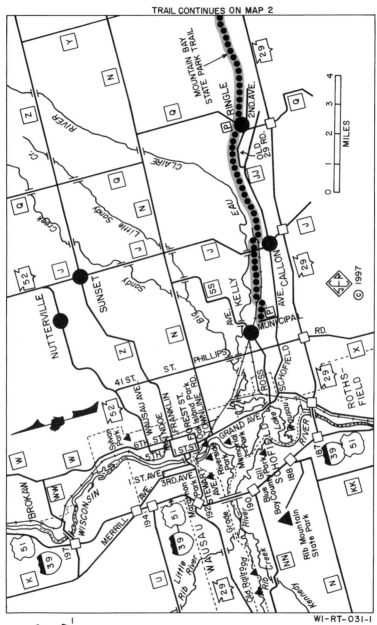

TRAIL CONTINUES ON MAP 2

WI-RT-031-I

MOUNTAIN BAY STATE PARK TRAIL (MAP I)
MARATHON, SHAWANO, & BROWN COUNTIES
83.4 MILES
SURFACE: SMOOTH CRUSHED GRAVEL

93

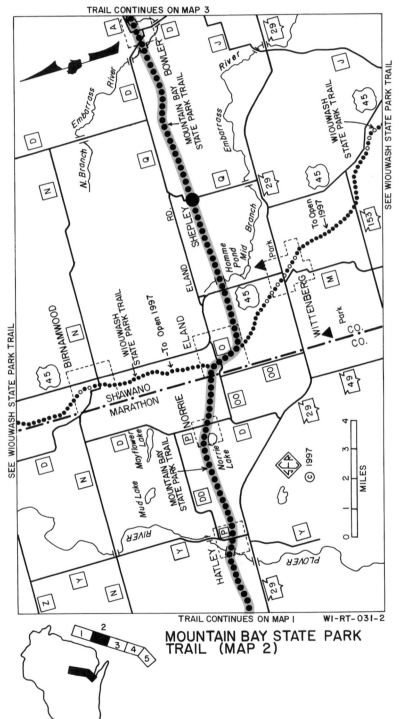

TRAIL CONTINUES ON MAP 3

TRAIL CONTINUES ON MAP I

WI-RT-031-2

MOUNTAIN BAY STATE PARK
TRAIL (MAP 2)

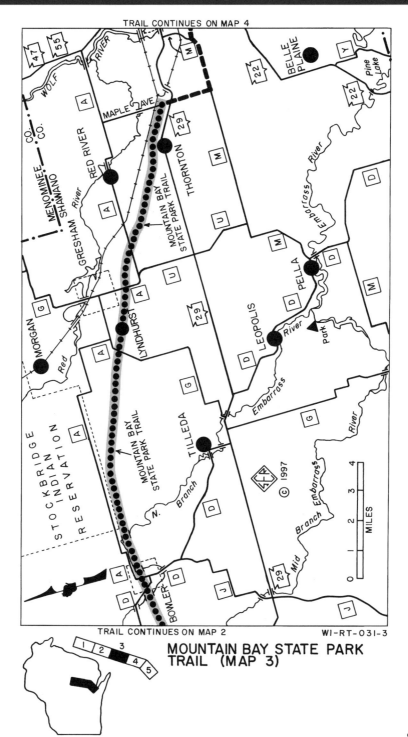

TRAIL CONTINUES ON MAP 4

TRAIL CONTINUES ON MAP 2

WI-RT-031-3

MOUNTAIN BAY STATE PARK
TRAIL (MAP 3)

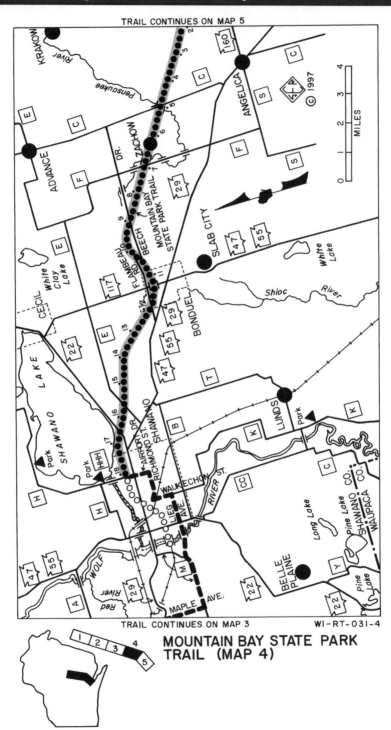

TRAIL CONTINUES ON MAP 5

© 1997

MOUNTAIN BAY STATE PARK
TRAIL (MAP 4)

TRAIL CONTINUES ON MAP 3   WI-RT-031-4

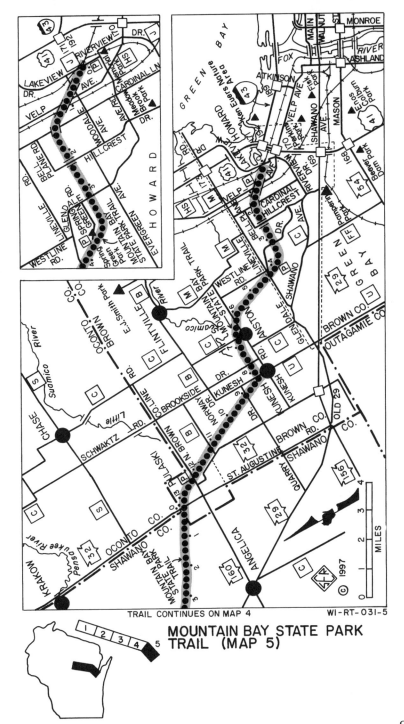

TRAIL CONTINUES ON MAP 4

WI-RT-031-5

MOUNTAIN BAY STATE PARK
TRAIL (MAP 5)

PECATONICA STATE PARK TRAIL
VICINITY: *Belmont*
TRAIL LENGTH: *10.5 miles*
SURFACE: *smooth crushed gravel*
TRAIL USE: 🪙 🪙 🚲 🛼 🏃 🚶 🐎 ⛷️ ➡️ 🏍️ ♿

The 10.5-mile Pecatonica State Park Trail follows the former Milwaukee Road railroad bed from Belmont to Calamine. Even though the trail has been around since the early 1980s, it was only in 1996 that a smooth crushed gravel surface was added for bicycle and wheelchair use. This unique trail is designed for a large variety of trail uses, including ATVs. Remember, mutual respect between all trail users can make the trail more enjoyable for everyone.

The scenery consists mostly of rolling farmland. The trail follows the Bonners Branch of the Pecatonica River for the entire length. Near Belmont, the First Capital State Park can be visited. Near Calamine, the Pecatonica State Park Trail intersects with the 47-mile Cheese Country Recreation Trail (This is not a State Park Trail, so a separate trail fee is required). Plans are in the works to extend the Pecatonica State Park Trail west to Platteville.

PARKING:
Parking is available in both Belmont and Calamine.

Dairy farms can be seen along the Pecatonica State Park Trail.

FOR MORE INFORMATION:
Tri-County Trail Commission
627 Washington St.
Darlington, WI 53530
608-776-4830

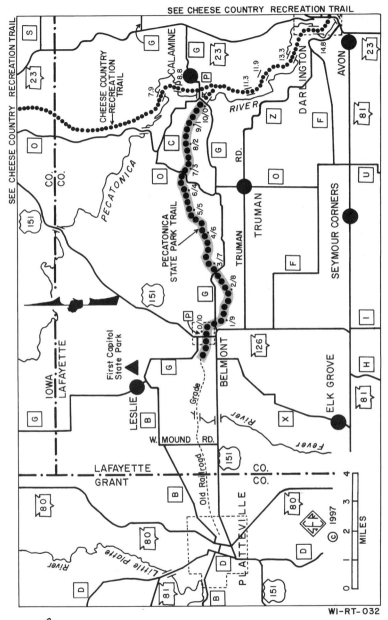

SEE CHEESE COUNTRY RECREATION TRAIL

PECATONICA STATE PARK TRAIL
LAFAYETTE COUNTY
10.5 MILES
SURFACE: SMOOTH CRUSHED GRAVEL

WI-RT-032

99

PINE RIVER RECREATION TRAIL
VICINITY: *Richland Center*
TRAIL LENGTH: *14.6 miles*
SURFACE: *smooth crushed gravel*
TRAIL USE:

The 14.6-mile Pine River Recreational Trail is located in Southern Richland County, between Richland Center and Lone Rock, and passes through the towns of Twin Bluffs and Gotham. The trail opened to the public in 1997. Its scenery consists of picturesque farmland and meadows between the forested hillsides of the Pine River Valley.

In Richland, the trail currently starts on Bohman Drive, near the Richland Square Shopping Center, along U.S. Route-14. The trail parallels the Pine River for nine miles southeast to Gotham. From Gotham, the Pine River parallels the Wisconsin River southeast for six miles to Lone Rock; U.S. Route-14 can be seen from a safe distance along this section of the trail. In Lone Rock, the Pine River Recreation Trail ends on Richland Street.

PARKING:
Parking can be found in Richland Center, Twin Bluffs, and Lone Rock.

The scenic valley of the Pine River Recreation Trail.

FOR MORE INFORMATION:
Richland County U W EXT. Service
1100 Highway 14 West
Richland Center, WI 53581
608-647-6148

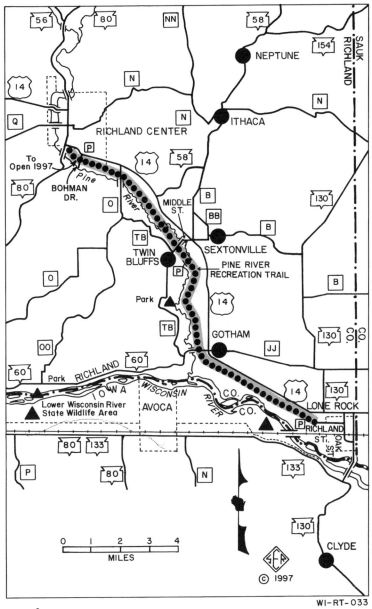

PINE RIVER RECREATION TRAIL
RICHLAND COUNTY
14.6 MILES
SURFACE: SMOOTH CRUSHED GRAVEL

RUSH LAKE TRAIL
VICINITY: *Rush Lake*
TRAIL LENGTH: *10.3 miles*
> *Green Lake County Recreation Trail, 2.0 miles*
> *Winnebago County Recreation Trail, 5.3 miles*
> *Ripon Recreation Trail, 3.0 miles*
SURFACE: *smooth crushed gravel*
TRAIL USE:

Currently, the Rush Lake Trail goes under three different names, in three different counties. At the moment, all three trails total 10.3 miles, between Berlin and Ripon. All three trails follow the former Chicago, Milwaukee, St. Paul, and Pacific Railroad grade. The trail opened to the public during the mid-1990s.

Rush Lake can be seen from the Winnebago County Recreation Trail in Winnebago County, near the town of Rush Lake. The scenery on the Green Lake County Recreational Trail section of this ride consists mostly of farmland and meadows, with spotted areas of woodland. In Berlin, the trail starts near Ripon Road and Industrial Park Road. Most of this part of the trail goes through a partially wooded valley. Just north of Ripon, near County Route-E and Locust Road, a parking lot is located on this end of the Ripon Recreational Trail. Future plans include extending this trail to Fond Du Lac.

PARKING:
Parking can be found near Berlin, along Willard Road, and near Ripon, on the corner of County Route-E and Locust Road.

FOR MORE INFORMATION:
Winnebago County Parks
500 East County Road Y
Oshkosh, WI 54901
414-424-0042

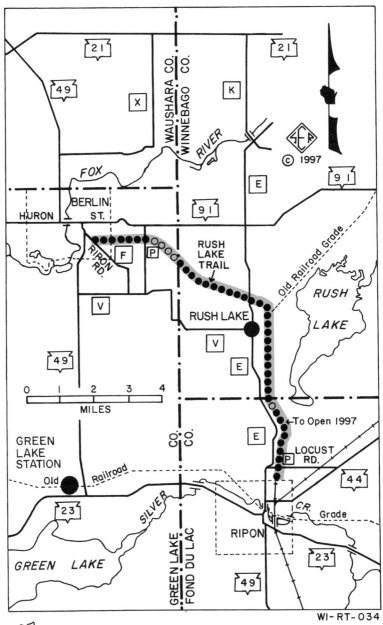

RUSH LAKE TRAIL
WAUSHARA, WINNEBAGO, &
FOND DU LAC COUNTIES
10.3 MILES
SURFACE: SMOOTH CRUSHED GRAVEL

WI-RT-034

103

WISCONSIN'S MAJOR BIKE TRAILS

BARABOO-DEVILS LAKE STATE PARK TRAIL
VICINITY: *Baraboo*
TRAIL LENGTH: *2.5 miles*
SURFACE: *asphalt*
TRAIL USE: $ 💲 🚲 🛹 🚶 📷 🐎 🛷 🏊 🏍 ♿

The 2.5-mile Baraboo-Devils Lake State Park Trail follows State Route-123 from Walnut Street, in Baraboo, to Devils Lake State Park. This trail was once a part of the 300-mile Wisconsin Bikeway.

Mountain biking can be enjoyed in Devils Lake State Park along a six-mile loop course. Before the glaciers over 10,000 years ago, the Wisconsin River once flowed where Devils Lake now lies. The blue lake and rocky bluffs make Devils Lake a very scenic Park.

PARKING:
Parking is available along the streets in Baraboo and in Devils Lake State Park (park entrance fee required).

Devils Lake in Devils Lake State Park.

FOR MORE INFORMATION:
Devils Lake State Park
55975 Park Rd.
Baraboo, WI 53913-0442
608-356-8301

Baraboo Area Chamber of Commerce
P.O. Box 442, Baraboo, WI 53913-0442
800-227-2266

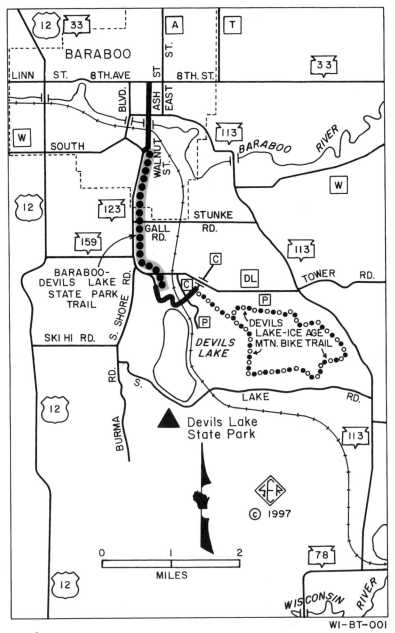

WI-BT-OOI

BARABOO-DEVILS LAKE STATE PARK TRAIL
SAUK COUNTY
2.5 MILES; SURFACE: ASPHALT

SUNSET TRAIL / HIDDEN BLUFF TRAIL

VICINITY: *Peninsula State Park*
TRAIL LENGTH: *5.8 miles*
SURFACE: *smooth crushed gravel*
TRAIL USE: 💲 💲 🚲 🚲 🥾 📷 🐎 ⛷ 🏊 🏍 ♿

The Sunset Trail follows the Green Bay coast through Peninsula State Park. The Hidden Bluff Trail follows Bluff Road, forming a loop with the Peninsula Trail. You'll see limestone rock formations along the coast. The southern part of the

Sunset Trail winds through Weborg Marsh, where wildlife is abundant. The Eagle Bluff Lighthouse Museum is a highlight along the Sunset trail, representing a very colorful part of Door County's past. If you have the time, you can experience a beautiful sunset from the appropriately named Sunset Trail. This very popular trail is hilly with curves, so it is highly recommended that cyclists travel the trail slowly. For a fee, you can also explore a network of mountain bike trails in Peninsula State Park.

PARKING:

If you're willing to pay the park entrance fee, parking can be found inside Peninsula State Park along the Sunset Trail.

Eagle Bluff Lighthouse in Peninsula State Park.

FOR MORE INFORMATION:

Peninsula State Park
P.O. Box 218, Fish Creek, WI 54212-0218
414-868-3258

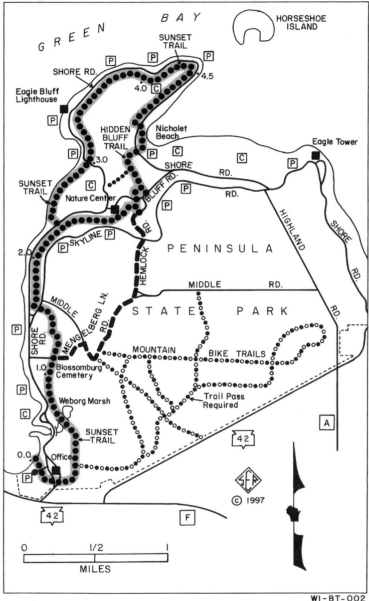

SUNSET/HIDDEN BLUFF TRAILS
DOOR COUNTY
5.8 MILES
SURFACE: SMOOTH CRUSHED GRAVEL

WI-BT-002

OLD PLANK ROAD TRAIL
VICINITY: *Sheboygan*
TRAIL LENGTH: *17.5 miles*
SURFACE: *asphalt*
TRAIL USE:

The 17.5-mile Old Plank Road Trail follows State Route-23 through Sheboygan County, from Greenbush to Shebogan. The Trail passes through Plymouth, Sheboygan Falls, and Kohler. This somewhat hilly and winding trail crosses Wisconsin's farmland. The Old Plank Road trail gets its name from the original wooden planks that made the road passable for horses and wagons during the mid to late 1800s.

From the west, the Old Plank Road Trail starts in Greenbush, where the Old Wade House State Park and Kettle Moraine State Forest are located (mile marker 0/17). From here, an off-road asphalt trail follows the south side of State Route-23. A short section of the trail (near mile marker 1/16) runs right on Julie Lane. In Plymouth, a short trail spur goes to a local city park (between mile markers 4/13 & 5/12). For a short distance near State Route-67, the Old Plank Road Trail follows the north side of State Route-23. From Mullet River to the east, the trail follows the south side of State Route-23 to Sheboygan. A second trail spur follows State Route-57 south to County Route-C, where parking is available in Plymouth (between mile markers 7/10 & 8/9). A third trail spur follows County Route-Y south into Kohler (mile marker 16/1). The east end of the Old Plank Road Trail is located on the east side of Interstate-43 with a parking area on Erie Avenue.

From here, you can reach Downtown Sheboygan and Lake Erie by following a combination of streets through Sheboygan, for four miles. A 1-mile off-road bicycle path follows the Lake Michigan Coast through downtown Sheboygan.

PARKING:
Parking is available in Greenbush, Plymouth (corner of State Route-57 & County Route C), Sheboygan Falls (corner of State Route-23 & Meadowlard Road), and Sheboygan (Erie Avenue east of Interstate-43).

FOR MORE INFORMATION:
Sheboygan Chamber of Commerce
712 Riverfront Dr., Suite 101
Sheboygan, WI 53081
800-457-9497

Old Wade House State Park in Greenbush

The Old Plank Road Trail follows State Route 23.

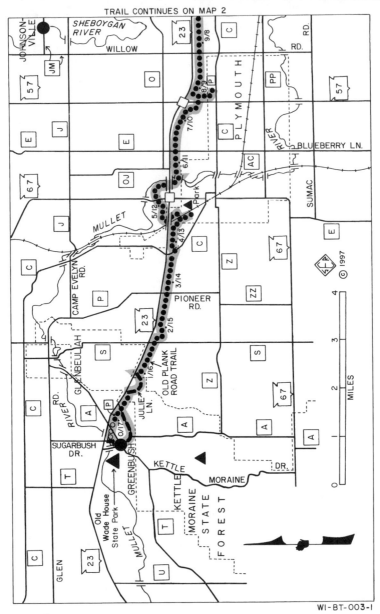

TRAIL CONTINUES ON MAP 2

SHEBOYGAN RIVER

JOHNSONVILLE

WILLOW

PLYMOUTH

BLUEBERRY LN.

Park

MULLET

PIONEER RD.

OLD PLANK ROAD TRAIL

JULIE LN.

GLENBEULAH

CAMP EVELYN RD.

SUGARBUSH DR.

GREENBUSH

KETTLE MORAINE

Old Wade House State Park

KETTLE MORAINE STATE FOREST

DR.

MILES

© 1997

WI-BT-003-1

OLD PLANK ROAD TRAIL (MAP I)
SHEBOYGAN COUNTY
17.5 MILES
SURFACE: ASPHALT

| 1 | 2 |

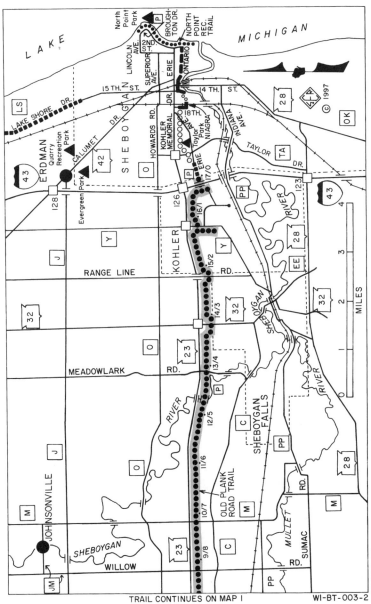

WI-BT-003-2

OLD PLANK ROAD TRAIL (MAP 2)

1 2

GREEN CIRCLE TRAIL
VICINITY: *Stevens Point*
TRAIL LENGTH: *24.0 miles*
SURFACE: *smooth crushed gravel, asphalt & streets*
TRAIL USE: 💲 💲 🚴 🚵 🚶 🏕 🐎 ⛷ 🛷 🚴 ♿

The 24-mile Green Circle Trail follows a combination of off-road trails and streets around the cities of Stevens Point, Plover, Whiting, and Park Ridge. The trail was built between 1990 and 1996.

This trail offers a wide variety of scenery. Tranquil river shores, streams, trees, and wildlife can be seen, as well as urban and suburban areas. The many views of the Wisconsin River are a major attraction of this trail. Another excellent stretch of the trail can be enjoyed in the northeastern part of Stevens Point, near the Stevens Point Municipal Airport. Other forms of recreation, such as canoeing, bird watching, family outings, or just plain solitude, are available in this area.

PARKING:
Parking is available along the Green Circle Trail in Stevens Point.

A winter scene along the Green Circle Trail.

FOR MORE INFORMATION:
Portage County Parks, County-City Building
1516 Church Street, Stevens Point, WI 54481-3598
715-346-1433

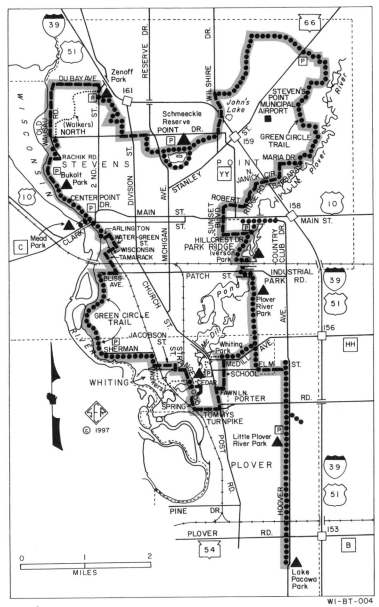

GREEN CIRCLE TRAIL
PORTAGE COUNTY
24.0 MILES
SURFACE: SMOOTH CRUSHED GRAVEL, ASPHALT,
& STREETS

WI-BT-004

WISCONSIN'S
UNIMPROVED
SURFACE
RAIL-TRAILS

BANNERMAN TRAIL

VICINITY: *Waushara County, Red Granite to 5 miles south of Wautoma*
TRAIL LENGTH: *7.0 miles*
SURFACE: *dirt*

TRAIL USE: 🔳 🔳 🔳 🔳 🔳 🔳 🔳 🔳 🔳 🔳 🔳

Waushara County Parks
Wautoma, WI 54982
414-787-7037

BUFFALO RIVER STATE PARK TRAIL

VICINITY: *Buffalo, Eau Claire, Jackson, & Trempealeau Counties; Fairchild to Mondovi*
TRAIL LENGTH: *36.4 miles*
SURFACE: *original ballast*

TRAIL USE: 🔳 🔳 🔳 🔳 🔳 🔳 🔳 🔳 🔳 🔳 🔳

Wisconsin Department of Natural Resources
Western Division, 1300 W. Clairmont Ave.
P.O. Box 4001, Eau Claire, WI 54701-6127
715-839-1607

CAT TAIL TRAIL

VICINITY: *Barren and Polk Counties; Almena to Amery*
TRAIL LENGTH: *17.8 miles*
SURFACE: *gravel*

TRAIL USE: 🔳 🔳 🔳 🔳 🔳 🔳 🔳 🔳 🔳 🔳 🔳

Polk County Information Center
710 Highway 35
South St. Croix Falls, WI 54024
800-222-7655

CLOVER CREEK TRAIL

VICINITY: *Price County; traverses the Chequamegon National Forest*
TRAIL LENGTH: *15.8 miles*
SURFACE: *dirt*

TRAIL USE: 🔳 🔳 🔳 🔳 🔳 🔳 🔳 🔳 🔳 🔳 🔳

Chequamegon National Forest
1170 S. 4th Ave., Park Falls, WI 54552
715-762-2461

FLORENCE COUNTY SNOWMOBILE TRAIL

VICINITY: *Florence County; traverses Nicolet National Forest*
TRAIL LENGTH: *32.4 miles*
SURFACE: *gravel*

TRAIL USE: 🔳 🔳 🔳 🔳 🔳 🔳 🔳 🔳 🔳 🔳 🔳

Nicolet National Forest
USFS-Florence Ranger District
HC 1, Box 83, Florence, WI 54121
715-528-4464

ICE AGE TRAIL

VICINITY: *Langlade County; traverses Langlade County Forest*
TRAIL LENGTH: *18.4 miles*
SURFACE: *gravel*

TRAIL USE: 💲 💲 ⛷ 🚴 🚶 🚂 🐎 ⛷ ➡ 🏍 ♿

Langlade County Forestry Department
P.O. Box 460, Antigo, WI 54409-0460
715-627-6236

IRON HORSE TRAIL

VICINITY: *Iron County; Manitowish to Frontier Campground*
TRAIL LENGTH: *55.0 miles*
SURFACE: *gravel*

TRAIL USE: 💲 💲 ⛷ 🚴 🚶 🚂 🐎 ⛷ ➡ 🏍 ♿

Iron County Forestry Office
603 3rd. Ave., Hurley, WI 54537
715-561-2697

KIMBALL CREEK TRAIL

VICINITY: *Forest County; traverses Nicolet National Forest*
TRAIL LENGTH: *12.0 miles*
SURFACE: *original ballast*

TRAIL USE: 💲 💲 ⛷ 🚴 🚶 🚂 🐎 ⛷ ➡ 🏍 ♿

Nocolet National Forest
Eagle River Ranger District
P.O. Box 1809, Eagle River, WI 54521
715-479-2827

NORTH FLAMBEAU CYCLE TRAIL

VICINITY: *Price County; traverses Chequamegon National Forest*
TRAIL LENGTH: *23.0 miles*
SURFACE: *dirt*

TRAIL USE: 💲 💲 ⛷ 🚴 🚶 🚂 🐎 ⛷ ➡ 🏍 ♿

Chequamegon National Forest
1170 4th Ave., South
Park Falls, WI 54552
715-762-2461

OLD ABE TRAIL
VICINITY: *Chippewa County; Chippewa Falls to Cornell*
TRAIL LENGTH: *17.0 miles*
SURFACE: *original ballast*
TRAIL USE: 🛇 🛇 🚲 🏍 🚶 🎿 🐎 ⛷ 🏊 🏍 ♿

Wisconsin DNR, Western Division
1300 W. Clairmont Ave., P.O. Box 4001
Eau Claire, WI 54701-6127
715-839-1607

OLIVER-WRENSHALL TRAIL
VICINITY: *Douglas County; Oliver to Wrenshall*
TRAIL LENGTH: *12.0 miles*
SURFACE: *dirt*
TRAIL USE: 🛇 🛇 🚲 🏍 🚶 🎿 🐎 ⛷ 🏊 🏍 ♿

Douglas County Forestry Department
P.O. Box 211, Solon Springs, WI 54873
715-378-2219

RILEY LAKE SNOWMOBILE TRAIL
VICINITY: *Price County; traverses Chequmegon National Forest*
TRAIL LENGTH: *23.0 miles*
SURFACE: *dirt*
TRAIL USE: 🛇 🛇 🚲 🏍 🚶 🎿 🐎 ⛷ 🏊 🏍 ♿

Chequamegon National Forest
1170 4th Ave. South
Park Falls, WI 54552
715-762-2461

TUSCOBIA STATE PARK TRAIL
VICINITY: *Barron, Price, Sawyer, & Washburn Counties; Park Falls to Rice Lake*
TRAIL LENGTH: *74.0 miles*
SURFACE: *original ballast*
TRAIL USE: 🛇 🛇 🚲 🏍 🚶 🎿 🐎 ⛷ 🏊 🏍 ♿

Tuscobia State Park Trail
Route 2, Box 2003, Hayward, WI 54843
715-634-6513

WOODVILLE TRAIL
VICINITY: *St. Croix County; Woodville to St. Croix County Line*
TRAIL LENGTH: *7.0 miles*
SURFACE: *gravel*
TRAIL USE: 🛇 🛇 🚲 🏍 🚶 🎿 🐎 ⛷ 🏊 🏍 ♿

County Clerk Government Center
1101 Carmichael Rd., Hudson, WI 54016
715-386-4600

WISCONSIN'S POTENTIAL BIKE TRAILS

Proposed Trail Name	Miles	End Points of Trail
Appleton-Hortonville Trail	11	Appleton-Hortonville
Ashland-Prentice Trail	85	Ashland-Prentice
Beloit-Caledonia Trail	13	Beloit, WI-Caledonia, IL
Beloit-Racine Trail	63	Beloit-Racine
Concept Trail	25	Sayner-Woodruff
Dresser-Amery Trail	16	Dresser-Amery
Fennimore-Woodman Trail	15	Fennimore-Woodman
Fond Du Lac-Campbellsport	16	Fond Du Lac-Campbellsport Trail
Fond Du Lac-Slinger Trail	35	Fond Du Lac-Slinger
Fox River Trail	4	Oshkosh Area
400 State Park Trail (Ext.)	30	Reedsburg-Merrimac
Gillett-Scott Lake Trail	89	Gillett-Scott Lake
Green Bay-Ahnapee State Park	33	Green Bay-Algoma Trail
Green Bay-Greenleaf Trail	13	Green Bay-Greenleaf
Green Bay-Manitowoc Trail	30	Green Bay-Manitowoc
Green Bay-Plover Trail	80	Green Bay-Plover
Hartford-Randolph Trail	39	Hartford-Randolph
Hudson-Merrillan Trail	110	Hudson-Merrillan
Janesville-Jefferson Trail	25	Janesville-Jefferson
Janesville-Palmyra Trail	29	Janesville-Palmyra
Ladysmith-Almena Trail	49	Ladysmith-Almena
Madison-Freeport Trail	45	Madison-Freeport
Madison-Janesville Trail	30	Madison-Janesville
Madison-Stoughton Trail	16	Madison-Stoughton
Madison-Sun Prairie Trail	15	Madison-Sun Prairie
Manitowoc-Fox Cities Trail	35	Manitowoc-Fox Cities
Manitowoc-Sheboygan Trail	25	Manitowoc-Sheboygan
Mauston-Wyeville Trail	23	Mauston-Wyeville
Mazomanie-Sauk City Trail	9	Mazomanie-Sauk City
Mellen-Bessemer Trail	33	Mellen-Bessemer

Proposed Trail Name	Miles	End Points of Trail
Monroe-Janesville Trail	34	Monroe-Janesville
Oconto-Nicolet Trail	21	Oconto-Nicolet
Oshkosh-Fox Cities Trail	6	Oshkosh-Fox Cities
Oshkosh-Ripon Trail	26	Oshkosh-Ripon
Portage-Wisconsin Dells Trail	17	Portage-Wisconsin Dells
Quarry Park Trail	2	Oshkosh Area
River Falls-Ellsworth Trail	11	River Falls-Ellsworth
Somerset-Chippewa Falls Trail	70	Somerset-Chippewa Falls
Stumpdodger Trail	51	La Farge-Wauzeka
Trego-Ashland Trail	55	Trego-Ashland
Urban Trail	13	Eau Claire Area
Wausau-Chippewa Falls Trail	90	Wausau-Chippewa Falls
Wausau-Marshfield Trail	40	Wausau-Marshfield
Wausau-Merrill Trail	19	Wausau-Merrill
Wild Goose State Park Trail (Ext.)	20	Fond Du Lac-Ripon
Wiouwash State Park Trail (Ext.)	34	Langlade County Area
Wiouwash State Park Trail (Ext.)	13	Oshkosh Area
Wisconsin Rapids-Vesper Trail	9	Wisconsin Rapids-Vesper

For more information on the developments of each trail, contact the Wisconsin Department of Natural Resources, P.O. Box 7921, Madison, WI 53707 or call 608-266-2621.

A 1940s-era passenger train — a predecessor to many of the bike trails that exist today.

FURTHER BICYCLE ROUTE INFORMATION

Wisconsin's Published Bicycle Maps

WISCONSIN (STATEWIDE COVERAGE)

Wisconsin Bicycle Map

Wisconsin Department of Tourism
123 W. Washington Ave.
P.O. Box 7976, Madison, WI 53707
800-372-2737 (IL,IA,MI,MN,WI)
800-432-8747 (National)

A set of 4 maps. Scale: 1 inch=4 miles.

A

APPLETON, COMBINED LOCKS, KAUKAUNA, KIMBERLY, LITTLE CHUTE, MENASHA, & NEENAH (FOX CITIES)

Your Bicycling Guide to the Fox Cities and Outlying Area

Fox Cities Convention & Visitors Bureau
110 Fox River Drive
Appleton, WI 54915
414-734-3358

Scale: 1 inch=2 miles

B

BOULDER JUNCTION

BATS, Boulder Area Trail System

Boulder Junction Chamber of Commerce, Inc.,
P.O. Box 286-B
Boulder Junction, WI 54512
715-385-2400

Scale: Large Scale

C

JANESVILLE

Experience Recreational Trails of Janesville, Wisconsin

City of Janesville, Leisure Services Division
17 N. Franklin St.
Janesville, WI 53545
608-755-3030

Scale: 2.5 inches=1 mile

D

LA CROSSE

La Crosse Bikeway Map

City Engineering Dept.
City Hall, La Crosse, WI 54601
608-789-7505

Scale: 1.25 inches=1 mile

E

MADISON

Madison Bicycling Resource Guide & Route Map

Madison Department of Transportation
P.O. Box 2986
Madison, WI 53701
608-266-4761

Scale: 1.8 inches=1 mile

F

MILWAUKEE

Milwaukee (Bike Map to come out in 1997)

Milwaukee County Parks
9480 Watertown Plank Rd.
Wauwatosa, WI 53226
414-257-6100

Scale: 0.75 inch=1 mile

G

RACINE COUNTY

Racine County Bicycle and Pedestrian Trails

Racine County Public Works
14200 Washington Ave.
Sturtevant, WI 53177-1253
414-886-8440

Scale: 1 inch=2 miles

H

WAUKESHA COUNTY

Bike Trails of Waukesha County

Waukesha County Parks and Planning Commission
1320 Pewaukee Rd.
Waukesha, .WI 53188

414-548-7790

Scale: 1 inch=4 miles

I

NORTH LAKES BICYCLE ROUTE

Stark, MN to Escanaba, MI (435 miles) Map

Adventure Cycling Association (formerly Bike Centennial)
P.O. Box 8308
Missoula, MT 59807-8308
800-721-8719

Scale: 1 inch=4 miles

Note: For current prices, contact the appropriate offices. Readers can obtain a free Wisconsin highway map by writing to the Wisconsin Department of Transportation, 3617 Pierstorff St., Madison, WI 53707-7713, or calling 608-246-3265.

Youth Hostels (U.S.A.)

AMERICAN YOUTH HOSTELS

733 15th St. NW, Suite 480
Washington, DC 20005
202-783-6161

ADDITIONAL YOUTH HOSTELS

The Hostel Handbook
722 St. Nicholas Ave.
New York, NY 10031
212-926-7030

Published Bicycle Maps in Wisconsin

U.S. Rails-To-Trails Guide Books

US GENERAL

700 Great Rail-trails: A National Directory of Multi-Use Paths Created from Abandoned Railroads.

Rails-to-Trails Conservancy, 1995, 1100-17th St. NW, 10th Floor, Washington, DC 20036.

A listing of trails for all 50 States. Maps not included.

CALIFORNIA

Rail-trail Guide to California, 1995, Infinity Press, P.O. Box 17883, Seattle, WA 98107.

Maps Included.

ILLINOIS

Illinois Rail-Trails, Rails-to-Trails Conservancy, 1992, RTC, 1100-17th St. NW, 10th Floor, Washington, DC 20036.

Maps Included.

Bicycle Trails of Illinois, 1996, American Bike Trails, 1257 S. Milwaukee Ave., Libertyville, IL 60048.

Maps Included.

IOWA

Bicycle Trails of Iowa, 1996, American Bike Trails, 1257 S. Milwaukee Ave., Libertyville, IL 60048.

Maps Included.

MINNESOTA

Biking Minnesota's Rail-Trails, Marlys Mickelson, 1998, Adventure Publications, Inc., P.O. Box 269, Cambridge, MN 55008.

Maps Included; book also shows some trails in Wisconsin.

OHIO

Biking Ohio's Rail-Trails, Shawn E. Richardson, 1997, Adventure Publications, Inc., P.O. Box 269, Cambridge, MN 55008

Maps Included.

PENNSYLVANIA

Pennsylvania's Great Rail-Trails, Rails-to-Trails Conservancy, 1994, RTC, 1100-17th St. NW, 10th Floor, Washington, DC 20036.

Maps Included.

WASHINGTON STATE

Washington's Rail-Trails, Fred Wert, 1992, The Mountaineers, 1011 SW Klickitat Way, Seattle, WA 98134.

Maps Included.

WEST VIRGINIA

Adventure Guide to West Virginia Rail-Trails, 1995, West Virginia Rails-to-Trails Council, P.O. Box 8889, South Charleston, WV 25303-0889.

Maps Included.

WISCONSIN

Biking Wisconsin's Rail-Trails, 1997, Adventure Publications, Inc., P.O. Box 269, Cambridge, MN 55008.

Maps Included.

NEW ENGLAND STATES (CT, MA, ME, NH, RI, & VT)

Great Rail-Trails of the Northeast, 1995, New England Cartographics Inc., P.O. Box 9369, North Amherst, MA 01059.

Maps Included.

Wisconsin Trails Index and Addresses

Wisconsin's Chamber of Commerces

Algoma	414-487-2041 & 800-498-4888
Ashland	715-682-2500
Bangor	608-486-4603 & 608-486-2356
Baraboo	608-356-8333 & 800-227-2266
Berlin	414-361-3636
Brodhead	608-897-8411
Brookfield	414-786-1886
Burlington	414-763-6044
Cudahy	414-483-5300
Darlington	608-776-4093
Dodgeville	608-935-5993
Eau Claire	715-834-1204
Elroy	608-462-8442
Fond Du Lac	414-921-9500
Fort Adkinson	414-563-3210, 888-733-3678 & 414-563-1870
Franklin	414-427-8989
Frederic	715-327-4836
Green Bay	414-437-8704
Greenfield	414-327-8500
Holmen	(See Onalaska)
Hortonville	414-779-6011
Janesville	608-757-3160
Jefferson	414-674-4632 & 414-674-4511
Juneau	414-386-4800
Kenosha	414-697-1234
La Crosse	608-784-4880
Lake Mills	414-648-3585
Madison	608-256-8348
Medford	715-748-4729 & 800-257-4729

Menomonee Falls	414-251-2430
Menomonie	414-235-9087
Milltown	715-825-2257
Milwaukee	414-226-4105 & 414-287-4100
Mineral Point	888-764-6894 & 608-987-3201
Minocqua	715-356-5266 & 800-446-6784
Monona	608-222-8565
Monroe	608-325-7648
Montello	608-297-7420
Mount Horeb	608-437-5914
Muskego	414-679-2550
New Berlin	414-786-5280
New Glarus	608-527-2095
Oak Creek	414-768-5845
Onalaska	608-781-9570 & 800-873-1901
Oshkosh	414-424-7700
Platteville	608-348-8888
Plymouth	414-893-0079
Pulaski	414-822-4400
Racine	414-634-1931
Reedsburg	608-524-2850 & 800-844-3507
Richland Center	608-647-6205 & 800-422-1318
Shawano	715-524-2139 & 800-235-8528
Sheboygan	414-457-9491
Siren	715-349-2273
South Milwaukee	414-762-2222
Sparta	608-269-4123 & 800-354-2453(Bike)
Stevens Point	715-344-1940
Sturgeon Bay	414-743-4456 & 800-527-3529
Superior	715-394-7716 & 800-942-5313
Sussex	414-246-3120

Tomahawk 715-453-5334

Verona 608-845-5777

Waterford 414-534-5911

Waukesha 414-542-4249

Waupun 414-324-3491

Wausau 715-845-6231

Wauwatosa 414-453-2330

Webster 715-866-7774

West Allis 414-321-7020

West Milwaukee 414-321-2585

West Salem .... (See Onalaska)

Wittenburg 715-253-3525

Join the Rails-to-Trails Conservancy

RAILS TO TRAILS CONSERVANCY MEMBERSHIP

To join the Rails-to-Trails Conservancy or give a gift membership to someone else, simply photocopy and complete this form. Mail it, along with the appropriate membership fee, to the address below.

Name _____

Street _____

City _____

State _____

Zip _____

Phone (include area code):

Home _____

Work _____

Membership level (Check the appropriate box):

    ☐ Individual Membership $18.00

    ☐ Family Membership $25.00

    ☐ Sustaining Membership $35.00

    ☐ Patron Membership $50.00

    ☐ Benefactor Membership $100.00

Enclose a check payable to Rail-to-Trails Conservancy and mail this form to:

    Rails-to-Trails Conservancy
    Shipping Department
    P.O. Box 295
    Federalsburg, MD 21632-0295

To join by using your Mastercard or Visa, call 800-888-7747.

BICYCLE SAFETY

Bicycle Safety

This article used with permission from Harvard Pilgrim Health Care, copyright © 1996.

Bicycling offers many rewards, among them a physically fit body and a pleasant means of transportation. But the sport has its hazards, which can lead to serious accidents and injuries. We have provided rules, facts and tips that can help minimize the dangers of bicycling while you're having fun.

Choose the right bicycle

Adults and children should ride bicycles with frames small enough to be straddled easily with both feet flat on the ground, and with handlebars that can be easily reached with elbows bent. Oversize bikes make it difficult to ride comfortably and maintain control. Likewise, don't buy a large bike for a child to grow into-smaller is safer.

Learn to ride the safe way

When learning to ride a bike, let a little air out of the tires, and practice steering and balancing by "scootering" around with both feet on the ground and the seat as low as possible. The "fly-or-fall" method-where someone runs alongside the bicycle and then lets go-can result in injuries.

Training wheels don't work, since the rider can't learn to balance until the wheels come off. They can be used with a timid rider, but the child still will have to learn to ride without them. Once the rider can balance and pedal (without training wheels), raise the seat so that the rider's leg is almost straight at the bottom of the pedal stroke.

Children seldom appreciate the dangers and hazards of city cycling. Make sure they understand the traffic laws before letting them onto the road.

Use this important equipment:

Headlight: A working headlight and rear reflector are required for night riding in some states. Side reflectors do not make the rider visible to drivers on cross streets.

Safety seat for children under 40 lbs.: Make sure the seat is mounted firmly over the rear wheel of the bike, and does not wobble when going downhill at high speed. Make sure the child will not slide down while riding. The carrier should also have a device to keep the child's feet from getting into the spokes.

<u>Package rack:</u> Racks are inexpensive, and they let the rider steer with both hands and keep packages out of the spokes.

Obey traffic laws

Car drivers are used to certain rules of the road, and bicyclists must obey them too. The following rules should be taught to a child as soon as he or she can ride a bicycle:

Make eye contact with a driver before entering or crossing lanes.

Signal and glance over your shoulder before changing lanes.

Watch for openings in the traffic stream and make turns from the appropriate lane.

When riding off-road, be sure you are on a trail that permits bicycles.

Before riding in the road, these rules should be practiced until they become habit and can be performed smoothly. Adults must set good examples-children imitate them regardless of verbal instructions.

Beware of dangerous practices

Never ride against traffic. Failure to observe this rule causes the majority of car-bicycle collisions. Motorists can't always avoid the maneuvers of a wrong-way rider since the car and bike move toward each other very quickly.

Never make a left turn from the right lane.

Never pass through an intersection at full speed.

Never ignore stop lights or stop signs.

Never enter traffic suddenly from a driveway or sidewalk. This rule is particularly important when the rider is a child, who is more difficult for a motorist to see.

Don't wear headphones that make it hard to hear and quickly respond to traffic.

Don't carry passengers on a bike. The only exception is a child under 40 lbs. who is buckled into an approved bike safety seat and wears a helmet, as required by law.

Passenger trailers can be safe and fun. Be aware, though, that a trailer makes the bike much longer and requires careful control. Passengers must wear helmets.

Find safe places to ride

Most cities have some bicycle-friendly routes, as well as some high-traffic areas that require skill and experience. It's safest to ride on secondary roads with light traffic. When choosing a route, remember that the wider the lane, the safer the cycling.

Get a bike that works with you

Skilled riders who use their bikes often for exercise or transport should consider buying multi-geared bikes, which increase efficiency while minimizing stress on the body. (These bikes may not be appropriate for young or unskilled riders, who may concentrate more on the gears than on the road.) The goal is to keep the pedals turning at a rate of 60-90 RPMs. Using the high gears while pedaling slowly is hard on the knees, and is slower and more tiring than the efficient pedaling of the experienced cyclist.

Have a safe trip!

Bicycle Helmets

Reprinted from July 1989 "Mayo Clinic Health Letter" with permission of Mayo Foundation, for Medical Education and Research, Rochester, Minnesota.

"It's as easy as falling off a bicycle." The adage has been around for decades. Unfortunately, it makes light of the potential for tragedy if you should take a serious fall while riding a bicycle.

With an increasing number of people riding bicycles on our streets and highways, the risk of injury - in particular, head injury—continues to rise. Each year, nearly 50,000 bicyclists suffer serious head injuries. According to the most recent statistics, head injuries are the leading cause of death in the approximately 1, 300 bicycle-related fatalities that occur annually. To a large extent, these head injuries are preventable.

Wearing a helmet can make a difference. Until recently, advocates of the use of protective headgear for cyclists found their stance lacked scientific support. But wearing protective headgear clearly makes a difference. Recent evidence confirms that a helmet can reduce your risk of serious head and brain injury by almost 90 percent should you be involved in a bicycle accident.

Bicycle riding is an excellent form of aerobic exercise that can benefit your musculoskeletal and cardiovascular systems. Make the investment in a helmet and take the time to put it on each time you ride.

What to look for in a bicycle helmet:

We endorse these guidelines for bicycle helmets recommended by the American Academy of Pediatrics:

The helmet should meet the voluntary testing standards of one of these two groups: American National Standards Institute (ANSI) OR Snell Memorial Foundation. Look for a sticker on the inside of the helmet.

1) Select the right size. Find one that fits comfortably and doesn't pinch.

2) Buy a helmet with a durable outer shell and a polystyrene liner. Be sure it allows adequate ventilation.

3) Use the adjustable foam pads to ensure a proper fit at the front, back and sides.

4) Adjust the strap for a snug fit. The helmet should cover the top of your forehead and not rock side to side or back and forth with the chain strap in place.

5) Replace your helmet if it is involved in an accident.

A Few More Bike Safety Tips

By Shawn E. Richardson

Rail-Trail Courtesy & Common Sense

1. Stay on designated trails.

2. Bicyclists use the right side of the trail (walkers use the left side of the trail).

3. Bicyclists should only pass slower users on the left side of the trail; use your voice to warn others when you need to pass.

4. Get off to the side of the trail if you need to stop.

5. Bicyclists should yield to all other users.

7. Do not use alcohol or drugs while on the trail.

8. Do not litter.

9. Do not trespass onto adjacent land.

10. Do not wear headphones while using the trail.

Emergency Tool-kit

When venturing out on bicycle tours, it is always smart to take along equipment to help make roadside adjustments and repairs. It is not necessary for every member of your group to carry a complete set of equipment, but make sure someone in your group brings along the equipment listed below:

1. Standard or slotted screwdriver.

2. Phillip's screwdriver

3. 6" or 8" adjustable wrench.

4. Small pliers.

5. Spoke adjuster.

6. Tire pressure gauge.

7. Portable tire pump.

8. Spare innertube.

9. Tire-changing lugs.

A Few Other Things

When embarking on an extended bike ride, it is important to give your bike a pre-ride check. To ensure that your bike is in premium condition, go over the bike's mechanisms, checking for any mechanical problems. It's best to catch these at home, and not when they occur "on the road." If you run into a problem that you can't fix yourself, you should check your local yellow pages for a professional bike mechanic.

When you are planning a longer trip, be sure to consider your own abilities and limitations, as well as those of any companions who may be riding with you. In general, you can ride about three times the length (time-wise) as your average training ride. If you have a regular cycling routine, this is a good basis by which to figure the maximum distance you can handle.

Finally, be aware of the weather. Bring plenty of sunblock for clear days, and rain gear for the rainy ones. Rain can make some rides miserable, in addition to making it difficult to hear other traffic. Winds can blow up sand, and greatly increase the difficulty of a trail.

About The Author

Shawn E. Richardson has worked as a cartographer for the Ohio Department of Transportation since 1988. He specializes in photogrammetry, the process of creating maps using aerial photography. He received his Bachelor of Science degree in environmental geography with emphasis on cartography from Kentucky's University of Louisville in 1985. A Kentucky native, Shawn has lived in Ohio since 1988.

Author Shawn E. Richardson

Shawn enjoys bicycle touring, and his excursions can last anywhere from a few hours to several days. Although he has biked back roads through many states, including the former 300-mile Wisconsin Bikeway, most of his touring has been on trails. He is an active member of the Ohio's Rail-to-Trails Conservancy and has belonged to the Columbus Outdoor Pursuits, the American Youth Hostels, and to the Louisville Wheelmen.

Biking Wisconsin's Rail-Trails is Shawn's second book. If you have questions or comments for Shawn, you can contact him by writing to:

Shawn E. Richardson
Biking USA's Rail-trails
PO Box 284
Hilliard, OH 43026-0284